Anxious Corporals

Anxious Corporals

Alan Morrison

Smokestack Books
1 Lake Terrace, Grewelthorpe,
Ripon HG4 3BU
e-mail: info@smokestack-books.co.uk
www.smokestack-books.co.uk

ISBN 9781916312128

Smokestack Books is represented by
Inpress Ltd

This book is dedicated
to my father, Andrew,

and to the memory of my
distaff grandfather, Harold –
two 'anxious corporals'

'Man was born a little below the angels, and has been descending into suburbanism ever since.'

TWH Crosland

'... in the inarticulate mass of the English populace he discerned the Conservative workingman as the sculptor perceives the angel prisoned in a block of marble.'

The Times obituary of Benjamin Disraeli, 18 April 1883

'We speak of the bad taste of our 'democratic' society. We mean by that a society whose tastes have become those of the people or... such as we usually expect of the people (namely, indifference to intellectual values, religion of emotion).'

Julien Benda

'Five and twenty ponies,
Trotting through the dark –
Brandy for the Parson,
'Baccy for the Clerk.'

Rudyard Kipling

'During the last war Arthur Koestler wrote... about what he called *'the anxious corporals'*... intelligent laymen in uniform. The war mixed us all up and the Armed Services... made such people seek each other out. So some highly-educated people discovered that intelligent laymen exist... They still exist, but the pressures to compartmentalise... lead us to forget them...'

Richard Hoggart

I

O this period of ectopic proletariat, common people
Misplaced in multiples of patchwork overlaps from cash-
Strapped and poverty-trapped working poor to tip-of-
The-slagheap grasping aspiration – O what hope for red roses
To grow among the thorns of red-top-hypnotised, populist-
Supporting proles, working-class Faragistes, Workington
'Gammons', purple-rinse reactionaries, blue collar
Conservatives, proletarian Tories (Old Benjamin Disraeli's
'Angels in Marble' coming back to haunt us through
Poltergeist psephologists, now Boris's blue collars, his batmen
Bootscrapers), who mostly think they're petit-bourgeois –
And thus *'called upon to hate each other'* as Christopher
Caudwell minted it in the Misty Thirties, and we still in
The death throes of a culture that started its protracted dying
Way back when – simply because they have mortgages and
Can afford to run motors (even two or three), or have bought
Their council houses, first steps up the property stepladder
Of Right-To-Buy-To-Let-To-Vet of thirty-plus years of purely
Material acquisition plus receipts but whose up-thrusting
Capital hasn't been matched by cultural accrual, no 'trickle-
Down' in interests and tastes (for *'footie'*, *'full Englishes'*,
Rusty builders' tea, imbecilic *'celebrities'*, tabloid tittle-tattle,
Hols in the Costa del Sol or Costa Brava, hangovers in
The Algarve, strictly bottled water while abroad and no
Fraternising with natives), still robustly un-ambitious,
Philistinism-tippling, prefer to stick to what they know,
Uncurious of everything they don't know, even hostile to it –
Knowledge, that great Unknown; potential for authentic
Cultivation of talents devastated by the haste to catch up
Capitalism's pace of ownership, shop-keeping or buying up
Properties, carpeted places of commodity-worship deep in
The pillared thickets of self-protective Villadom (hives
Of conventional values, private nativism, perfumed mores)
Premium-bond-and-mothballed suburbia, fetishist shrines
With vast flatscreens as altarpieces for faiths in artificial
Things (aspidistras transplanted by satellite dishes), religions

Rooted wholly in this world (whose quotidian gods are
Terrible to behold in all their dreadful blandness), and some
Vague evangelism for self-aggrandisement through gadgets
Of ergonomic advantage, visceral acquisitiveness for all
Things tactile, instantly titillating, spiritual impoverishment
Through conspicuous consumption of superfluous products
Of built-in obsolescence, human flourishing undernourished,
Forever deferred like cheap credit, higher purchase purgatory,
Appetites sampled and amplified in surround sound,
Magnified in higher definition with better special effects,
Spectacle at expense of authenticity, eviscerated of soul,
Ersatz tsars of idiots' lanterns (some mutely tormented by
Intrusive thoughts zapped-in by television and advertising),
Repressed aspirations as to ever properly exploring
Their personalities pickled as specimens in aspic of plastic
Replication, preserved forever half-formed in formaldehydes
Of commodification, stuffed manikins enthroned in morbidly
Obese armchairs, fat sofas of false satisfaction, trappings
And appliances purely for plasma-display; so social
Anthropologists might diagnose that human personality
Captive under capitalism has a built-in obsolescence every bit
As inhibiting as the objects and products onto which
Advertising copywriters – cropped poets of salesmanship,
Corporate-sponsored, poetically parasitic – project
Personalities through anthropomorphising spiel (almost a
Spell) in order to make them irresistibly pettable to
The consumer population – the cut-price capitalist cult
Of commodity-fetishism; against this travestied backdrop it's
Easy to forget that mere decades ago the working and lower-
Middle classes comprised armies of aspiring self-improvers,
Intellectually inquisitive and culturally acquisitive
Knowledge-hungry thought-guerrillas, unarmed paper armies
Scavenging for knowledge off-campus from academies,
Rusticating outside rusting institutions, such demand was
There for mutual improvement overturning the unintelligent
Margarine of *'yellow press'* matter, tabloids' butter-
Substitutes, *'Sunny'* Harmsworth's *Daily Mail* (inveterate
Barometer of lower-middle-class Villadom), *Tit-Bits*,

Answers, *Readers' Digest*; an incipient curiousness
Outstripping supply of tepid potboilers and self-help
Pamphlets stamped, borrowed and battered from libraries –
Incubators for lowbrow dog-end knowledge – by blue collar
Browsers on lunch breaks, abridged indulgences to grease
Semi-engaged minds hungry for something unidentified,
Faint tastes half-articulated; cheap pulp in peach prose to help
The unhappily employed escape themselves in short-sleeved
Evenings of post-supper sleepiness (*'postprandial'* to more
Silver-spooned phrasemakers), keep the empty-pocketed
Temporarily happier in their penury; but their appetites kept
Ripening and pressing through orange peels of colportage
Impressed on them to keep them in their places and something
Had to come and fill up this rupturing gap in the market for
Self-improvers and autodidacts: step in Pelican, which joined
Penguin's orange millions, and whose insuperable blue spines
Sprang up in 1937 like spring forget-me-nots, or a bruise
Of bluebells in the cool dark woods of bookshops, non-fiction
Reinforcements, factual, didactic, erudite reads that came to
Mobilise ambitious and curious brains above their allotted
Stations to different altitudes of thought through a belated but
Timely redistribution of knowledge, each paperback just
Sixpence, price of a cheap packet of cigarettes – *Capstan
Navy Cut* non-filters in blue liveries, *Passing Clouds* in
Primrose-pink packets, *Army Club ('The Front-Line Cigarette'*
Which *'steadies the nerves'*), or *Sweet Caporal* – all in
Elegant oblong boxes; *'Who would have imagined'*, founder
Allen Lane opined *'That, even at 6d, there was a thirsty
Public anxious to buy thousands of copies of books on
Science, sociology, economics, archaeology, astronomy and
Other equally serious subjects?' Who* indeed? Who would
Have thought it, who would have bought it? The public did,
Eagerly! *'Good Books cheap'* went the Pelican strap-line.
Lane had both a commercial and democratic eye, what
Average Joe wouldn't buy books for self-improvement if so
Readily available and cheaply priced? Rows on rows of sky
Blue spines, temptingly Promethean, greeting all and sundry
In every high street *Woolworths*, sixpenny spines mutely

Triumphant amidst ten-a-penny tacky bric-a-brac, plaster
Ornaments and plastic commodities of built-in obsolescence
Like so many customers' hollow occupations – now
Knowledge, low-hanging knowledge of highbrow
Blackberries – or rather, blueberries – was affordable for
The ordinary person, the autodidactic proletariat, and lumpen
Unemployed, no penny-dreadful pulp, no low-hanging fruit
Of knowledge, but superior branches of knowledge, for Lane's
Promethean aim was that such knowledge should not
Be the plum preserve of the privileged but the jam
Of the masses, the ambrosial substitute for the mind
Of the miner, milkman, factory-hand; scholarly manna for
The working man and woman, to help them gradually
Transcend the limited mental horizons of their predetermined
Places on the lower bowl-scrapes and spaces of pyramidal
Capitalism's economic caste system – bonds of those
Untouchables spruced with patchouli-oil and honest toil about
To undo themselves, long-unarticulated talents, untapped
Aptitudes and intellectual appetites to rupture across pages,
Ranges of pages, print-archipelagos, insatiable itches for
Mutual-improvement, pure and simple, mental, intellectual,
Moral, spiritual, in spite of permanent advertising pitches
Of capitalist society, consumerism's emphasis on prices at
Expense of substance, its inauthentic auspices of shops, pubs,
Tobacconists, boutiques, those public escapist emporiums
Open for corpses' pennies to be spent in to dope up spent
Spirits with cheap plastic raptures, Bakelite objects, pills,
Fillips, potions, opiates, consciousness-substitutes, punctuated
By optional chapels, meeting halls and Labour Clubs – self-
Help portals to replenish empties of *entfremdung*-wrung
Souls, pariahs of the species-essence at their own expense,
Easily manipulated supplicants in the purgatories of *'strip-
Lighting together with imitation chandelier'* where *'notice
After blazing notice winks, glows, or blushes luminously ...'*,
Its salesmen and floorwalkers so many sharp-suited high
Priests of retail, Pharisees of receipts for worshippers of hire
Purchase and higher purposes *'with their neat ready-made
Clothing, shiny... shoes, well-creamed hair... ready smiles'*...

II

Pelican – so named by serendipity when publisher Allen Lane
Overheard a man at a bookstall mistakenly ask for *'one of
Those Pelican books'* when he meant Penguin of course –
Tipped its first title off the production line in pale blue spine:
George Bernard Shaw's *The Intelligent Woman's Guide to
Socialism, Capitalism, Sovietism and Fascism* – a sixpenny
Salvation of mankind, to paraphrase its author's enraptured
Pitch, though aimed more titularly at the scholarly housewife-
Cum-homebound bluestocking now emancipated from
Aspirins and thin domestic magazines after years yearning for
Something illuminating, more revealing and enlightening than
Glossed gossip, something authentic, similarly stimulating to
The mind and spirit as swilling tea-leaves was to the formica-
Palmed clairvoyant or the hair-curlered gossipers of well-
Scrubbed doorsteps and tongues of tar soap who talked
Of a ubiquitous *'They'* who were *'reported to order that out
Of every ten contraceptive sheaths manufactured, one should
Be punctured; and 'They' put bromide in servicemen's tea, to
Reduce the sexual urges'*, pop a *'pessary'* in if you can't hold
With those Dutch caps, and butter wouldn't melt, the price
Of butter etcetera etc... shouldn't smoke so much but she has
To have a lift of some sort, a fillip, something with a fuming
Tip so she can fume away, release a gasket, although
The smoke makes her feel like an old crock, too much rouge
From hours spent at the steaming mangle – the wrought-iron
Granny Smith-green Norahammars Bruk makes her look
'Grock-like', a shocker, a Mrs Judy Punch, chin clamped,
Grotesque, prognathous as a Hapsburg, which Richard
Hoggart described in his groundbreaking monograph-cum-
Polemic-cum-poem *The Uses of Literacy: Aspects of
Working-Class Life, with Special References to Publications
And Entertainments* (Chatto 1957, went on to become an
Iconic Pelican by '58): *'The lines on the face of an old
Working-class woman are... magnificently expressive – but
...hard earned... a face with a scaly texture... the lines... have
Grime in them'*; Hoggart staggered into Grand-Guignol:

'The hands are bony claws covered with densely lined skin,
And again the dirt is well-ingrained...: years of snatched
Washes... in cold water, have caused that. The face has two
Marked lines of force – from the sides of the nose down to
The compressed lips; they tell of years of 'calculating"...
Shaw's unapologetically didactic paperback sold surprisingly
Quick, became a common staple of many households'
Bookshelves, planting the tri-band blue-white-blue Pelican
Livery firmly in its new domestic setting; for Lane smelt
A proletarian appetite for appropriation of broader branches
Of knowledge, ontological grounding in capitalism's two-
Dimensional hoarding-propped pop-up pretend-world (little
More than *'a film set'* to Christopher Isherwood, author
Of the filmic novel *Prater Violet*), its rented world of spirit-
Puncturing employment and mind-dulling shadow play,
Which smelt faintly of greasepaint and turpentine through
The masking fumes of smog, smoke, damp, petrol, patchouli,
Mould, rust – halitosis of industry and its pollutants spread
Rapaciously through over-production amidst under-
Consumption; something had to come and exorcise the sour-
Smelling complacency of the economically emptied Thirties'
Rut in thought and inaction that coated that decade like
A mould, the cultural chic of acedic reflection contrasted with
'The newspapers' scintillating confusion of day-to-day
Events', as Lane wrote; an unlikely paper relief column
Comprising old hands, such as ex-drapers' assistant and clerk-
Turned-upcoming polymath and futuristic writer, HG Wells,
The better-heeled though no less idealistic RH Tawney –
Author of the tectonic plate-shifting anti-capitalist Twenties
Treatise, *The Acquisitive Society* – and Beatrice Webb, came
To the intellectual rescue, and all those writers, socialists
Of various sorts, slightly fusty but still sharp-minded Fabians
And far-sighted gradualists, partly due to Pelican's co-
Founding editor's staunch socialist politics, the exotically
Named VK Krishna Menon, a vegetarian tea-topping teetotal
Who knocked back a hundred cups of the warm and wet stuff
A day, sleeping only two hours per night – a veritable
Mad Hatter of the publishing trade, and part-throwback to

The Seventeenth Century hermitic pamphleteer-cum-aesthete-
Cum-herbalist-cum-Puritan-cum-aspiring angel, Roger Crab;
And by no means as gas-mad and raging as that vegetarian
Teetotal Austrian-born lance corporal of the Bavarian Reserve
Who won an Iron Cross for bravery and a Black Wound
Badge for being maimed in the cause of duty, only to go on –
After failed artistry, long-term unemployment, dosshouses,
He, bohemian once, flip-flopped through flophouses – to
Forge a ruthless regime which, among legion abominations,
Stitched black triangle badges on the striped shirts
Of the unemployed, homeless, mentally ill, disabled and lame,
Then extemporised a European apocalypse... (And I am
The grandson of an anxious corporal of the Buffs who fought
In North Africa against Rommel's sand-capped Afrika Korps,
Risked his life to save a wounded officer who in any case later
Died, all un-witnessed, was captured and kept in a Prisoner
Of War camp for four years of the war, tortured for trying to
Escape several times, bashed over the head with a rifle butt,
Made to stand out in the snow naked, whose nerves never
Recovered, demobbed for perceived incapacity, in his
Declining years, predeceased by my green-ink grandmother,
Was shocked into Huntington's *huis clos* in a damp Brighton
Terrace on Balfour Road he nicknamed *'Stalag VII-A'*, partly
Affectionately, since during his imprisonment he'd learned
German as a means of nourishing his mind and keeping
Himself sane, and had a fascination for things German for
The rest of his life; and I am also the son of anxious corporal
Whose nerves had been scarred permanently from having
Almost been burnt to death as a baby after his dressing-gown
Caught fire accidentally, who, though scholarly, gentle,
Sensitive, suited for the clergy, joined the Royal Marines at
Seventeen, beret green as he was green, not on a commission
For he'd been deemed too lacking in self-confidence to be an
Officer, in spite of his classical education – so he was thrown
Into the ranks and waded up to corporal but couldn't
Accomplish more, then on his return to Civvy Street was
Recruited by the civil service, spent the next twenty years in
Administrative work, a desk-bound white-collar corporal)...

III

Sigmund Freud's *Psychopathology of Everyday Life* and
Virginia Woolf's *The Common Reader* (her attempt to
Empathise with non-experts' perceptions of literature) sold
Out their first print runs in days; Pelicans weren't simply
Cheap and accessible but were also portable, easily curled
Softbacks that could slip into back pockets – books as well as
Browsing minds were being mobilised en masse, this was
A literature movement, mute permanent revolutions were
In continual motion on racks in every *Woolworths*; Pelicans
Were selling in tens then hundreds of thousands, then in
The millions, unlikely titles became bestsellers – like HDF
Kitto's *The Greeks*, or OR Gurney's *The Hittites*; Lane's
Long-vision of providing an invaluable – though sometimes
'Heavy going' – *'Everyman's'* archive for voracious readers
Of varying interests had been realised and evenly valorised
For everyone, even the insolvent, establishing bedsitter-
Universities for tin-rationed scholars, cardiganed indigents,
Aspiring radicals, so-called *'culture-vultures'*, blackcoated
Autodidacts and many a blue-collar scholar who would forgo
A pack of gaspers for a fat paperback of analysis and facts
(Though the perfect combo was a book and some Woodbines –
harp intake of facts accompanied by much well-informed
Harrumphing), abracadabra of abstract rabbits out of hats;
And various creative thinkers could find artistic sustenance,
Inventive nutrition, soul-nourishment, in easily digestible
Grains of aggregate learning – sky-blue spines for blue-sky
Thinking, not simply that type limited to advertising or
Marketing boardrooms, but open to the unemployed
Philosopher, or philosophical *'shirker'*, the sky-blue thinker,
Opting for rustication from conventional society to spend time
Expanding the mind – as Anthony Aloysius St. John Hancock,
Sweater-wearing bedsit self-improver forever stuck on
The opening paragraph of Bertrand Russell's *History of Western
Philosophy*, on the cusp of gasping comprehension,
In the rut of Railway Cuttings in sempiternal East Cheam...
Who would have thought Pelican's sky-blue spines could put

Such a spell upon the public, both chalk-striped Civvy Street
Of the Blitz and khaki servicemen through the war-torn
Forties that they would help to socially educate and enlighten
Them to vote in Clement Attlee's Labour Party with an
Avalanche, trouncing valiant Winston...? With some help
From Victor Gollancz' Left Book Club and the then-recently
Republished and unexpurgated *The Ragged Trousered*
Philanthropists which was passed around khaki readers keen
To lap up any printed matter – almost akin to the pamphlets
And tracts of Winstanley and Lilburne proselytising to
Roundhead rank and file converting many to Levellers and
Diggers, who marked themselves out with black and sea-
Green feathers... Something was miraculously built up amidst
The Blitz, the rubble, bombs, doodlebugs and obliterated
Buildings, a death-defying effort of mind and spirit pollinated
A populace with seeds of self-educating instinct, and so
The war was also a bonanza of intellectual ambition met with
Timely bombardments of books, cheaply-priced cherries
Of scholarship and apples of polemic ripe for picking by
Scrumping self-improvers cloyed by pulp colportage
Of toothbrushed spivs, their cheap detective novels with
Saucy-postcard covers and semi-pornographic double
Entendre titles – *Lady Don't Fall Backwards* and the like –
Such appetite for improvement in the face of random death
Was noted by a gratified George Orwell during the war years,
Most impressed by this mass dash for reading matter which
'Would have been regarded by the general public as
Impossibly highbrow a few years back' – war was a raw
Reminder of blink-and-you'll-miss-it civilisation and culture,
Unappreciated in peacetime, prized when imperilled; cheap
But unexpurgated sources of thought-nourishing, intellectual
Provisions for the curious Joe on the street, the modern
Obscure Jude just 6d away from advancing his knowledge
Into realms of gold autodidactism (though here one risks
Viewing things through rose-tinted spectacles of *'middle-class*
Intellectuals with strong social consciences' who had *'for*
A long time tended to see every second working-class man as
A Felix Holt or a Jude the Obscure' according to the Gospel

Of Hoggart – who had more than a hint of Hogarth in his
Empirical name, himself a working-class scholarship boy,
Who scorned rhetorically: *'How many major English writers*
...over-emphasise the salty features of working-class life?'
Though Hoggart himself wasn't immune to the odd spot
Of salting with images straight out of Hardy's grim Wessex
Mythologies: *'The local quality of... life of a working-class*
Man is well-illustrated by the way he will... trudge... across
Town with a handcart... transporting a sixth-hand kitchen
Table... One is reminded of Tess of the d'Urbervilles *moving*
From one valley to another... seeming, to herself, to move
From one country to another'; yet Hoggart noted *'even a*
Writer as astringent... as George Orwell never... lost the habit
Of seeing the working-classes through the cosy fug of an
Edwardian music-hall'; for completely different reasons
'There is a wide range of similar attitudes running down to
The folksy ballyhoo of the Sunday columnists... who... quote
With admiration the latest bon mot *of their pub-pal 'Alf"*)...

IV

Pelican would be sharp-beaked, audacious, sprightly motif
For a democratisation of nous, new spectacled meritocracy –
No more would higher reaches of human brambles be special
Preserve of the privileged; these blue-striped paperback
Prometheans perfect antidotes to the daily scourge of spurious
Red-tops, Allen Lane diagnosed the public *'wanted a solid*
Background to give some coherence to the newspaper's
Scintillating confusion of day-to-day events'; and Pelicans
Were numbered, so past titles accidentally skipped could be
Retraced, and catalogued; ambrosial books for the labouring
Classes, scholarly blue collars and doorstep-scrubbing
Bluestocking aspirin-spirited housewives, not only cheap but
Portable, Pelicans slipped perfectly into back pockets of many
An autodidact, blue-and-white-striped passports to
Hemispheres of self-improvement... Another catalyst behind

Pelican was WE Williams, so-called *'Pelican Bill'*, crumpled
Proctor who was also at the vanguard of this educative
Revolution and, like Lane, evangelical for the democratising
Of culture, who had ties with the Workers' Educational
Association (founded with some spare housekeeping money
By one Albert Mansbridge, carpenter's son, articled clerk-
Cum-evening tutor in industrial history and typing, and
Mostly self-taught 'gentleman' of Gloucester), and, as Director
Of the Army Bureau of Current Affairs, made sure during
The war the Pelican imprint kept a prime place amid
Regimental reading matter, thus many servicemen thrived on
Elevations of thought they conveyed, devouring everything
Available on every subject, sophomoric pilots, especially keen
Shadier readers, lower-middle-class gentlemen-rankers
(Kipling's *'cleanly bred, machinely crammed'*, well-
Camouflaged grammar schoolboys and graduates), privates
With privet-clipped accents, of rusticating mystique,
Squaddies with degrees or other certificated qualifications,
Mobilised from the shabby-genteel, those on *'the shivering
Verge'* of gentility as George Orwell phrased his own
Background; more common in times of war due to mass
Conscription from all stratums – though in the main most
Middle-class rankers would be picked up quickly for
Promotion to officers, unless some of them politely refused
Commissions, among them Privates (Ralph) Vaughan Williams,
(Ivor) Gurney, (David) Jones, (Randall) Swingler,
And, attempting to escape his desert-deep reputation which
Implacably preceded him, aircraftsman TE Shaw (Lawrence
'Of Arabia')... But most of the readerships were among less-
Educated working-class rankers or those who'd been
Promoted up a couple of rungs, and those back in Civvy
Street who'd staggered the ladder from blue collars to
Blackcoated workers, clerks, or *'writers'* as minor clerical
Workers were called (*'clerk'* a variant of the French *'clerc'*,
Meaning a *'literate'* person, *'clergyman'* or *'scribe'* – and
Used with deliberate etymological charge to denote
'Intellectuals' by Julien Benda in his iconic 1927 polemic

La Trahison des Clercs translated as *The Treason of*
The Intellectuals) hence the crossover of meanings in the term '
Clerical'; and weren't clerks descended from the Worshipful
Company of London Parish Clerks of Clerks' Well, later
Clerkenwell...?, corporals of the clerical hierarchy, white-
Collar corporals (those rooks that roosted in offices, once
Wood-panelled nooks, clerkly rookeries, jackdaws
Of counting-houses scratching at parchments with feathered
Quills – or more like crows since often partitioned and solitary
(Which precluded solidarity), perched at desks-like-lecterns
On the sub-branches of the upper-working and lower-middle
Pecking orders, who could trace their occupational ancestry
Back almost exclusively through Victorian yellowbacks and
Edwardian novels: from Charles Dickens' Philip 'Pip' Pirrip
(*Great Expectations*), Bob Cratchit (*A Christmas Carol*), and
Wilkins Micawber (*David Copperfield*); through George and
Weedon Grossmiths' petit-bourgeois fusspot Charles
Pooter (*The Diary of a Nobody*); George Gissing's unrefined
Christopher Parish (*The Town Traveller*), down-on-his-luck
Writer-cum-clerk Edwin Reardon (*New Grub Street*); HG
Wells's George McWhirter Fotheringay (*The Man Who Could*
Work Miracles); EM Forster's out-of-work anomic clerk
Leonard Bart brought to the brink of occupational catastrophe
(*Howard's End*); JB Priestley's languid Harold Turgis, clerk
For veneer-and-inlay company Twigg & Dersingham (*Angel*
Pavement); Shan F Bullock's Robert Thorne (*Robert Thorne:*
The Story of a London Clerk); Graham Greene's Conrad
Drover (*It's a Battlefield*); and John Davidson's 'Thirty Bob
A Week' clerk occupying cramped rooms of a poem...) – not
Quite the class of '*knowledge workers*', qualified
'*Professional thinkers*', though one JS Harrison in an 1852
Pamphlet on the theme noted the intrinsic '*mental effort*'
Of office work, of a more '*improving nature than manual*
Work', induced in the blackcoated worker a tendency to
'*Anxiety*' and '*a more susceptible and sensitive state of mind*
Than rougher and less mental pursuits' – and Houlston noted
Continuous routines of clerking were '*wholly incompatible*
With impatience, indolence or nervous agitation of mind',

Euphemisms, one presumes, for artistic temperaments;
Houlston also cautioned clerks against bookish habits, 'mustard-
Plaster' fiction – novels being *'hurtful to the mind... as
Habitual dram-drinking is to the body'*; *Houlston's Handbook*
For clerking novices was indispensible in nurturing one's
Character, practising occupational self-discipline, not
Submitting to the perilous temptation of attempting to escape
One's predetermined station – in any case, promotions
Weren't so much upwards as sideways, particularly in railway
Clerking, lateral delegations littering lost-property shops
Of opportunities, upper echelons of executive positions pretty
Much closed shops to all but those catapulted from public
Schools – apart from exceptions to rules, upstarts with
Propensities at *'pushfulness'* whose poverty of prospects
Served as self-propelled springboards of motivation to scrape
Occupational promotion, hop up stepladders of pipedreams;
The majority were sapped of willpower too much to grope up
The swampy slopes of promotion, often fell into the pitfall
Of *'satisfactoriness'*, working too long in a groove from
Which they'd never be able to escape; desk-clamped
Dreamers' dim smiles departmentalised, talents eternally
Retarded by the slow-track shuffling of papers, even
Their glazed eyes amalgamated, dreams rationalised – for
Theirs was work of *'the dullest routine character'*, as David
Lockwood put it in *The Blackcoated Worker – A Study In
Class Consciousness* (1958); the painstakingly round-
The-clock automatic expertise of book-keeping and
Correspondence, filing, cashiering, and all the other tasks
Of envelope-and-foolscap purgatory; so much scope in an
Occupation with such small scope for promotion or self-
Improvement for extra-occupational accomplishments through
Private pastimes, particularly artistic – painting, music, prose,
Poetic compositions, pursuits perceived specially appropriate
To the *'educated gentleman'* (or, to be more precise,
The publicly schooled) rather than to the self-educated lower-
Middle-class white collar, in spite of his aspirations; and yet
Many were ever buckers of convention in these regards, there
Having been a long historied association between the clerical

And literary, many writers had worked as clerks, also called,
Ironically, '*writers*' – such luminaries as Thomas Love
Peacock, Charles Lamb, George Hull, Charles Dickens,
Arnold Bennett, Julius West, James 'Bysshe Vanolis'
Thomson, Richard Le Gallienne, Arthur Morrison, Howard
Spring, Guy de Maupassant, H.G. Wells, Herbert Read, John
Drinkwater, Franz Kafka, Knut Hamsun, Paul van Ostaijen,
Douglas Oliver, RC Sherriff, JB Priestley (at Helm & Co.,
A wool firm in the Swan Arcade, Bradford), Richard Hoggart –
All of whom kept themselves in writing by working
The daily drudge in offices performing clerical or secretarial
Chores – not least Florence Margaret 'Stevie' Smith, doomed
Old maid of Palmers Green whom – before earning renown
For her quirky poems-cum-nursery-rhymes – patched
Together her brittle autobiographical *Novel on Yellow Paper*
(1936) from the typed thoughts of a disentranced secretary
Called '*Pompey*'... But schooling in such delicacies as fine
Art, poetry and music were not seen as necessary qualities for
'*The tough world of commercial negotiation*' (even if sundry
Dreamer-clerks had slim volumes of verse up their sleeves or
Slivers of novels tucked into the folds of their blotting pads
Discreetly as metal files in prison cakes – as Mark Rutherford
Wrote of the working-class protagonist in his novel
Revolution in Tanner's Lane: '*Not to the prosperous man... is
Byron precious, but to the poor wretch, say some City clerk,
With an aspiration beyond his desk, who has two rooms in
Camberwell*'; the clerk had to make himself '*indispensable*' if
He wanted to get on, and in the counting houses clerks and
Their employers worked closely, cementing a sense of mock-
Commonality across ranks and grades while permanently
Retarding any common consciousness across all clerks, what
Might have been mythically called *clerk consciousness* –
Whose status, in any case, differed from one establishment to
The next, so too the salary scales, hence the class-sense
Of each clerk who also had his own price; but could clerks
Have much bargaining power when their '*profession*', if it
Could be called such, lacked any clear classification? '*...with
Better qualification and grading will come greater craft*

Consciousness... No authoritative body has ever bothered to
Put down in black and white what qualifications should entitle
A person to call himself a clerk' – though blue collars might
Cite a lack of masculinity... Male clerks' virility was
Emasculated by double-edged *'Respectability'*; male office
Workers had smoother and more manicured hands than was
The norm for their gender, unmanly hands of slimmer fingers –
For an occupation that was widely stigmatised as *'unmanly'*
By manual man – phalanges of *'gentlemanliness'*, and had
More feminine qualities for which they were remunerated in
'Salaries' as opposed to *'wages'* (though pecuniarily similar),
Much of which was donated daily to upper-middle-class
Employers effectively gratis in return for such implicit
Perceptual privileges as *'Respectability'*, an invisible sign or
Status-signature worn proudly as a transparent badge on
Broadcloth – as opposed to manual workers' fustian – lapels,
So too by synecdoche were they softer in speech and
Expression than the rougher and brasher working class, and
O they'd do almost anything to avoid the roughness
Of the outside associated with the glassy-skinned, pallid,
Ginger children of the working classes, guttersnipes,
Scallywags, urchins, *chavi*... Those on the shivering verge
Of gentility, the shabby-genteel, were politely taciturn,
Inoffensive, sometimes ineffectual, painfully attentive to
Etiquette, even perceived as effete and fussy by those on
Whose doormats they'd never wipe their feet, shunned as
'Posh' and *'snobbish'* by grubbier neighbours aggrieved by
Their own inverted snobberies, yet themselves down-at-heel,
Only pretending otherwise – another difference; always
Dressing to impress (themselves, mostly) – clothes weren't
Just worn for necessity of climate – rags against rinsings –
But also for symbolic effect; as one disenchanted clerk put it
Bitterly in *The Clerk's Journal* in 1890: *'Foolish parents wish*
To see their sons in broadcloth instead of fustian; they think
A clerk is a gentleman and an artisan not' – but not all
Aspects of keeping up appearances had a price-tag attached:
'The ideal of the gentleman in the second half of
The nineteenth century, being... defined as a state of mind and

A corresponding mode of conduct... an inexpensive luxury',
Wrote David Lockwood, as if depicting the precepts
Of chivalry; though *'gentlemanliness and respectability could
Become curiously confused in the lower-middle-class culture'*,
The admixture of the two concepts *'acted as a powerful social
Control over any intransigence or insurrection on the part
Of the clerk'*; this hankering after *'prestige'* simply heaped
A further hurdle before realisation of clerical consciousness,
In spite of *'the penurious condition'* of clerks – employers
Exploited this relationship, *'and great expectations frequently
Came to nothing'*; yet the white collar insatiably itched
Against the chafed neck-skin of the clerk towards
A continuous need to be scratched by social graces, or at least
Their illusion: for *'a clerk's duties... are of a more
Enlightening and improving nature than manual work'*; clerks
Were *'of decent address and gentlemanly habits, patient and
Long-suffering, not given to 'noisily insisting upon
Their rights"* – they were possessed of *'delicacy when
Requesting an advance of salary, not unnaturally believing...
Their employers ought to recognise their merits'*... But by
Such subtleties of conduct were clerks eminently exploitable
And taken for granted: *'Gentlemanliness... interpreted as an
Avoidance of disagreements about pecuniary matters within
A relationship'*; together with *'the privilege of appearing
'Gentlemanly' in appearance'* and *'mannerism... within
The office, must be counted... the possibility of mixing with
The sons of gentlemen'*; prestige was everything, even at
The price of *"respectable'* salary, *'clerking'* was perceived as
A social advance but one *'purchased at the cost of diminishing
Income"*; by the early Thirties incipient proletarianisation
Of clerking was perceptible when *'Klingender established
That one out of every three London clerks under the age of
Twenty-five came from a working-class family'*, while greater
Heterogeneity was found in *The Social Survey of Merseyside*
(1934): *'The great majority... are... children of shopkeepers,
Shop assistants, insurance agents, school teachers, or... come
From the skilled and semi-skilled sections of the working
Class'*; according to occupational classifications of the Forties,

Office workers, clerks, shorthand-typists, book-keepers,
Secretaries came firmly in Class 4, about halfway up the scale
Of social stratification – just below them, salesmen and
Commercial Travellers (5), then shop assistants (6), foremen,
Supervisory workers, policemen, non-commissioned officers
In the armed forces (7) – those corporals anxious and others
More accustomed to their positions; by the Fifties it was
Found *'one out of every two clerks stems from the home of*
A manual wage-earner'; the clerking classes were similarly
Stratified in Forties Sweden, as uncovered by Croner who
Surveyed the broader composition of the Swedish *'salariat'*,
Called *Angestellten* – almost translating as Angst class –
That were positioned as the upper-working/lower-middle class
Of that markedly more equal kingdom; the social marginality
Of clerks could be exacerbated to anomie since many took
Spouses from other classes, whether slightly above or beneath
Their stations – unlike most other professions they were not
'Endogamous', had no qualms about class-miscegenation...

V

Keeping up appearances primarily for themselves, shabby-
Genteel in denial of their shabbiness, but in a social limbo
Of status ambiguity, neither quite one thing nor the other,
Clinging on the hinges of the half-open door to rosier
Prospects, as one Hugh McCleod aphorised so aptly with
A Northern accent: *'Distrusted by the masses' yet despised by*
The 'classes' – though their nearest cousins, the upper-
Working-class, aped some of their manners and habits; unlike
The full-blooded working class who found their sense
Of security and belonging in the neighbourhood they grew up
In, roots in concreted community, the lower-middle class was
More clannish, created psychical and atmospheric domestic
Sanctuaries, their homes private reposes of respectable
Claustrophobia, barely spoken shibboleths and eyeballed
Taboos, reflection, contemplation, temperance, repression,

Enshrouded in pot-plant shadows, aspidistra'd introspection
Scoured by nervous tonics and colic tripe – cosseted
Neuroticism chronic as the tea which acted as its conductor,
Poured from curved spouts of warped black teapots by bone
China wrists of anxious, rattly aunts, wives and mothers who
Spoke like broken crockery; above all, proud, too proud to
Ever accept *'charity'* of any kind, or to quite reasonably claim
Anything back from the State, like rates rebates, and most
Shameful of all, the temptation of getting things on
The *'never-never'*, *'tick'* or credit – euphemised as *'hire
Purchase'* – while drink was the most vulgar and lascivious
Of all vices, but not always entirely rinsed out from
Commercial Travellers Christian Associations or YMCAs
Whose atmospheres could *'bleach the Christianity out of
A man'* when sundry imbibing lapsed chapel-goers caroused
Around and regaled novices, rooms-less clerks and drapers'
Assistants *sans* regular digs, with lewd anecdotes, only to
Strike down any Christian remonstrance by name-calling as
'Salvation Armyists' or chastising them for their Quakerish
'Racketiness'; chapels and meeting houses hotbeds for mutual
Improvement in-between prayers, as were Clarion Clubs,
Cooperative Unions, Corresponding Societies, Workers'
Guilds, and Social Reform League get-togethers (while
Friendly Societies, such as the Clerks Associations, served as
Labour bureaus by way of exchange, and provided
Rudimentary welfare, child and widow relief for sick and
Unemployed clerks – numerous white-collar workers were
Susceptible to pulmonary tuberculosis due to working such
Long deskbound hours in stuffy offices, poorly ventilated
Breeding grounds for germs, incubators for *tubercule bacilli*);
Consumption cropped up episodically in clerkish accounts –
'White plague' of white collars... *'Where do they, like the flies,
Go in the winter of their lives? Do they simply, like old
Soldiers, fade away... or have they realised by then that
Clerking is a hopeless job, and taken up stone breaking or
Something more lucrative than their own calling?'* Quite
Possibly, since many clerks were *'downwardly mobile to
Various kinds of manual work'* – these were termed

'Skidders'; those clerks who rose to higher ranks were
Overwhelmingly from more prosperous social backgrounds
Rather than from the *'lower-blackcoated and working-class
Backgrounds'...* But there was some lower-middle-class
Dissent from codes of decorum and conformity: if not quite
A tendency to hedonism, there was an effortful fumbling for
A greater sense of freedom which expressed itself in a sub-
Culture of cycling – by pennyfarthing or tandem – and
Socialism, and *'flouting of respectable norms... among clerks,
Teachers, shop assistants, telegraphists... white collar youth'*,
Hankering after some commonality with hitherto shunned and
Marginalised working classes; contrary to much received
Evidence pockets of the lower-middle-class did dabble in
Dialectics of socialist societies, while white collar unions
Tended to be more class conscious and politically militant
Than manual workers' unions – though bruised by begrudging
Blue-collared brothers for their *'flabby, jelly-fish' attributes
Of 'gentility'* (*The Clerk's Journal*, 1890) – the National
Union of Clerks was both radical and deprecating of its own
Membership base – as per one of its president's speeches, in
1915, which called the clerk *'a docile being... the first hope
Of suburbia... and the last hope of the master class during
Strikes. If he has given the world any other impression than
That of a professional Judas for Capitalism it is the vague
Idea... he has created the demand for five-a-penny cigarettes,
The half-penny press, and guinea Macintoshes'* – a damning
Epithet! More and more were other energies and ideas
Impinging on lower-middle-class *'Respectability'* and
Religious instruction (though that strata jealously guarded its
'Respectability' in the face of all change, no matter how
Gradual), and *'always... exhortations to throw aside
The artificial flower of 'Respectability''*, wrote Richard Price,
*'Fell upon the stony ground of what Bernard Shaw (himself
A clerk) termed the highest possible development of
The qualities of 'sheepishness... docility... cowardice''*;
Political thought, mostly socialist, and *'popular rationalism
Fed on the RPA cheap classics'*, inculcated a more
Intellectually curious and culturally acquisitive white-collar

Youth; the march of mutual improvement was proving
Formidable, if insurmountable, and the quest for knowledge-
Acquisition an increasingly obsessive pursuit of the mentally
Restless clerk – as one WJ Brown, a Post Office clerk from
Battersea, illustrated in his recollections – circa 1910 –
Of studying for an hour before breakfast, rowing a boat in
Battersea Park, then walking to work, there to *'spend a good
Deal of the day exchanging ideas with his workmates, talking
Being permitted'*, then after work spent all the remaining
'five Glorious hours of freedom' among heaps of books at
The local library lapping up prose on politics, science and
Religion – every nerve of his organism engaged in and
Greased with an eagerness for knowledge, his steaming
Energies firing on all cylinders and pistons in a race
Of scholasticism – his was the knowledge-generator
Generation immediately preceding disciples of Pelicans...
Clerks' vices were *'false consciousness'* and *'snobbishness'*,
In spite of being financially close to the working classes and,
Like them, contractual labour, the salaried clerk was
Perceived as being *'of different clay'* to manual workers, those
Who worked with their hands and were depicted as *'Canute-
Like... standing out against the irresistible tide of
'Proletarianisation' in spite of essentially being part of
The proletariat in that they too were 'propertyless''* – clay
Canutes; railway clerks, the more down-at-heel of their breed,
Were more easily radicalised due to poor pay and conditions,
Retarded upward mobility, kept up appearances like the rest
But more prone to protest against limitations of their stations
And to strike if needs be, more unionised than most, and keen
To emphasise appearances can be misleading, as noted in
The Railway Clerk, October 1917: *'The idea that everybody
Who 'looks nice and dressy' is a snob and lacking in class
Consciousness is neither in accord with logic nor facts.
Some Individuals give one the impression that to be 'advanced
Thinkers' and class conscious, one must wear a dirty collar,
Shabby clothes and a general air of slovenliness'* – in other
Words the typical bohemian or saunterer; of all blackcoated
Workers, railway clerks were the most overwhelmingly from

Working-class backgrounds (whereas commercial and
Banking clerks were more likely to come from lower-middle-
Class origins), many being sons of railwaymen, hence many
Members of the Railway Clerks Association were in
Simpatico with claims of the National Union of Railwaymen:
*'The study of... trade unionism among railway clerks can only
Lead to a rejection of the common stereotype of the clerk, and
... an awareness of the... variations in class consciousness...
That stereotype obscures'*; but many members of the RCA
Were resistant to the union's pro-Labour politicisation
Believing this would put off potential members with more
Conservative opinions from joining it, especially if to do so be
Perceived as tripping palm-in-palm with manual workers –
Even in the most proletarian-oriented of clerical unions was
A ninety per cent seam of small-c-and-big-C Conservatism;
But when it came to collective self-interest, the RCA was
Radical, as in its robust campaign against *'uncompensated
Sunday duty'* – by 1906 the Workmen's Compensation Bill
Satisfied many of their demands; while blue collar strikers
Were ever in danger of industrial blacklisting, unionised
Blackcoats were stalked by *'red-ink records'*, and could be
Boycotted by *'character-notes'* – blacklists of blackcoats!
Although, as Lockwood pointed out, *'The past traditions of
Railway service had all been on the side of producing
A blackleg rather than a striker'*; a correspondent
Of *The Railway Service Journal*, 1919, expressed blackcoats'
Circumspection of strikes, always last resorts in industrial
Disputes: *'The strike idea was... something wonderful, but
Fearful; a monster hideous and repulsive;... awful and
Unthinkable. Despite all this it was a grim necessity'*; war
Terms like *'going over the top'* were melodramatically
Intoned by railway clerks in the event of a strike; *'During
The early Twenties the old fears of the clerk as a weak link'*
Where unions were concerned was still rawly felt, bruising
Bugbear of blackcoat blacklegging; but much solidarity
Through sympathetic striking was expressed by colliery
Clerks, railway clerks, docks clerks and all those working in
Close proximity to manual workers; *'1913 saw the first*

Lockout of clerks who refused to blackleg in the big dock
Strike', and *'in July 1915 some fifty-seven clerks struck over*
A case of victimisation at Nobel's Explosives Factory'; during
The Depression-hit Thirties the NUC membership became
More politicised than any other clerical union, much page-
Space in its *Journal* given over to debates on political hot-
Topics of the day, and a recrudescent tendency of delegates
Supporting the Communist Party in its path to Labour
Affiliation; the NUC was also *'active in denouncing Fascism*
At home and abroad' contributing 'to the International Solidarity
Fund Money earmarked for Spanish workers, and as late as
1943... was still donating funds to the International
Brigade' – this political aspect polarised: many clerks
Remained reticent to join the union *'because of its left-wing*
Policy'; such attitudes corroborated by its London secretary as
Quoted in *The Clerk*, February 1939: *'one of the principal*
Reasons for the smallness of the union... is this continual
Foisting of political opinions down people's throats';
Nevertheless, there was a clear revival in industrial unionism
In the mid-to-late Thirties; the biggest purely clerical union
Was the Civil Service Clerical Association which, despite
Representing Government employees, was a militant trade
Union with close ties to the Labour Movement, formed post-
1918; the 1919 railway strike caused the association to clarify
Its *'policy on trade-union solidarity'* due to many clerks being
Bribed to be blacklegs; WJ Brown cautioned strike-breaking
Members blacklegging would rebound against them under
A possible future Labour Government, and well *'he knew...*
Railway leaders had been called Bolsheviks and Anarchists.
The Press which described them by these names was owned
And controlled by people whose interests were diametrically
Opposed'... At the core of the CSCA was a group of radically-
Inclined assistant clerks, the union often perceived as *'Red'*,
Its general secretary nicknamed *'Bolshevik Brown'*, though
His militancy was on a cause-by-cause basis rather than
A cause in itself; with salary cuts in 1931, Brown spoke out
Defiantly against government: *'Lenin once said... you might*
Judge when the capitalist order of society was reaching

Collapsing point when... driven by the stress of its own
Internal position to drive the petty bourgeois down to the level
Of the proletariat'; in 1945 the general Secretary of the TUC
Expressed to Congress what he observed as bouleversement:
'*The old-time snobbery of the blackcoated worker has tended*
In recent years to give place to a sort of inverted snobbery
Which causes the manual worker to regard with... disdain
The clerk and office worker'; the CSCA had been
Foreshadowed by the Assistant Clerks Association protest
Group which formally affiliated to the Labour Movement in
1918 – its mouthpiece, the incredulously named *Red Tape*
(Though it might have been called *Pink String*), its last
Political Act, a motion at the annual meeting of 1920,
'*That a grant of fifty pounds from the political fund be made to*
The Daily Herald', a paper founded for the common reader in
1910 by the printers' union, the London Society
Of Compositors, intended as a permanent daily on behalf
Of the Labour Movement, though unaffiliated, funds for
Which were raised by dockers' union leader, Ben Tillett,
Along with TE Naylor, and George Lansbury who'd become
One of the Herald's longest-serving editors, then later, leader
Of the Labour Party 1931–35 (through unpredictable twists
And turns, changes in ownership, by 1964 the paper would be
Rebranded as *The Sun*, and post-1969 be bought by rapacious
Australian tycoon Rupert Murdoch under whose business
Thumb it would become more rampantly populist, Labourite
In the Seventies but switching political allegiance to
Thatcherite Toryism in the deregulating Eighties, instrumental
In the generational brainwashing of swathes of the working
Classes, tempting them into competition, one-upmanship,
Property-worship and self-interest, helping to fragment
Proletarian identity, fracture solidarity – still the red rag is
Read today by vast reserves of 'blue collar Conservatives')...

VI

As for the *'aristocracy' of clerks'*, the bank employees,
Their unionisation was *'respectable'* as would be expected
For an *'ultra-middle-class group of workers'*, in the guise
Of the Bank Officers' Guild, which grew exponentially
With germ of amalgamations, depersonalisation of office
Relations, *'and by the anxieties raised by the disappearance
Of old grades'*; emphasis of the unflatteringly abbreviated
BOG had always been on negotiations and *'moral suasion'*
Rather than strikes, its class-distance from other trade unions,
Explicit: *'The guild is a trade union... with a new ideal –
Co-operation... The guild has never departed from... pacific
Aims... We roundly repudiate the assumption that in having
A class consciousness we have necessarily class antagonism'*,
But middle-class quietism of bank clerks was engrained in
Their DNA, rinsed in Conservatism, the guild had stayed
Neutral during the 1926 General Strike, acting as mediator in
The national dispute, but was conscious of the sacrifices
Of manual workers as acknowledged by its President: *'Now
That we have forgotten these little inconveniences of getting
Up earlier... walking a few miles extra to and from the office,
May we... spare a sympathetic thought... for the miner... his
Ways of living... and the risks he runs in his daily round, for
He also is a man'* – then to a nitpicking letter of July 1926
Which, with almost neurotic precision, excerpted the parts
Of an editorial in *The Bank Officer* that had unsettled
The letter-writer, now reassurance-seeking: *'A speaker at
The recent Annual General Meeting called for an increased
Spirit of class consciousness among bank clerks. I do not
Clearly understand what class consciousness is, though it is
A phrase much used by persons whose proposals include
The violent and bloody upheaval of our social system'*; there
Were some dissenting voices among the ranks of banking
Clerks, such as another letter-writer expressing disgust at
The reactionary default of most of his fellow bank workers: '
*Am I for ever to witness bank clerk Fascists helping to break
The General Strike or bank clerk Special Constables waiting*

To wipe up a few hunger marches?' The president
Of the BOG was at pains to reassure members just after
The General Strike there was no necessity to submit to
Their kneejerk call to strike out the strike clause altogether:
*'I do not care how Bolshevik a man may be in his ideas or
How far he looks ahead. Under no known conditions today
Could you envisage a national strike of bank clerks'*; so
The motion was lost – Bolshevik bank clerks indeed! Despite
The 1931 cuts, bank clerks' salaries were still relatively better
Than manual workers' and other clerks', but this was an
Advantage bank clerks bore on their brows and shoulders
More as guilty burdens: *'The fear that clutches at our bowels
Is that we... get paid more for our jobs than those who do
Work like ours outside banks. This fear is the most paralysing
Of all. I have seen it in men's eyes and... gestures. This it is
Which chiefly prevents them from 'standing up to
The brandishing of the employers' bludgeons'* – the *'militant
Attitude'* was on the ascendant and became more concentrated
With the merging of BOG and the SBCA under the umbrella
National Union of Bank Employees; other reports showed
A fifty-fifty split between reactionary and radical or *'TUC-
Minded'* members – as one anonymous source aphorised in
Olfactory metaphors: *'50% are absolutely opposed to
Anything that smells of TUC. Not all the scent of NUBE
Pamphlets can counteract the smells of... TUC Garlic. These
Gentlemen... hold their noses and say we will have nothing to
Do with NUBE so long as it has anything to do with
The TUC'*; keeping the gastronomic figurativeness, unions,
Being such large conglomerations, were always going to be
Goulashes of varying meat-and-vegetable sensibilities,
Melting pots of jostling interests and opinions; post-1918,
Trade unionism was perceived as *"an infection going round
The country like influenza', the cost-of-living was soaring,
The social distance between blackcoat and fustian had...
Diminished in the war-time community... new, aggressive
Unions, such as the National Union of Clerks, were invading
The local government field'*; suggestions the National
Association of Local Government Officers should register as

A union were dismissed by members since it already had
Union functions, *'power'* was bandied about as something
The union required, power spelt out as *'funds'* – as a letter in
Possession of a Mr Spoor from one of the delegates present
Sketched it: *'What were the funds of this Association?
(Voices: '2s 5d' and laughter.) Talk about a lightning strike.
(Renewed laughter).'National Union of Local Government
Officers. National strike begins at 10 a.m. by the members
Downing pens. It ended at 10.47 a.m. owing to... exhaustion
Of the strike fund.' (Laughter)'* – point wittily taken, motion
To register as a union, defeated, *'as was a motion that a ballot
Of the members be taken'*; this reticence put off potential new
Members: *'Demobilised soldiers were avoiding NALGO and
Joining what they considered... 'real'... unions... The General
Strike had put trade unionism in bad odour with the middle
Classes'*... Striking depended on an individual worker's
Circumstances as much as on his political convictions, and
Those *'on the bread line often had the choice made for them
By necessity of putting food on the table... While for
The association itself, striking also depended on how much
They had in the 'kitty''*; unionisation and clerkdom had never
Been easy bedfellows: *'The degree to which clerks have
Participated in... associations for strike-breaking, or
Fascist Movements, is... unknown... All have... tended to eschew
The strike weapon as... instrument of collective bargaining'*;
There was also much opportunism amongst blackcoated
Associations in that clerks often joined trade unions *'not out
Of sympathy with the Labour Movement but in order to
Protect themselves from 'pressure from below''*; there was an
Ideological disconnect, a variability in allegiance to Labourite
Aims among various types of clerk, thus inconsistency in
Policy across blackcoated unions; hence why so many clerks
Acquired reputations as blacklegs: *'In the pre-1914 years, as
In the inter-war period, clerks were... recruited as Special
Constables... they also figured in the Army Supplementary
Reserve'*, and in the strike-breaking Middle Classes Union;
While CL Mowat in his *Britain Between the Wars* (1956)
Argued *'The British Union of Fascists recruited mainly from*

This class of the population', Lockwood found no evidence of
This any more than '*members of the lumpenproletariat*' or
'*Retired army personnel*' – nonetheless, some blackcoats had
Mutated into blackshirts... Bank and railway clerks' attitudes
Towards the Labour Movement differed widely due to
Forming the '*aristocracy and proletariat of the blackcoated
World*' respectively; '*while bank clerks came mainly from
The lower middle classes, great many railway clerks were...
From... homes of railway workers*' and his '*self-respect was...
Bound up with his standing in the railway community.
Perhaps just because of his blackcoat, and the suspicions... it
Aroused, he felt... he had to 'prove' himself in the eyes of
The railwaymen who worked by his side and to whom he was
Often related*'; class had always been defined in terms
Of '*market-*' and '*work-situation*', but of equal sociological
Concern was the "*prestige*' dimension of social stratification'
Upon which much hinged for the clerk – '*The charge
Of 'false' class consciousness... frequently levelled at
The blackcoated worker*' was '*grounded in the assumption...
Manual workers and clerks share the same basic market
Situation*' of '*propertyless, contractual labour*' even if
The clerk, '*really a proletarian in a white collar*', was '*blinded
To... his class position by... obdurate snobbery*' and '*incurable
Pretentiousness*' – Lockwood agreed with Marx and Weber
That '*property and lack of property are the basic categories of
All class situations*' and that '*a lack of sustained bargaining
Power, job insecurity, and... social immobility... were
Concomitants of propertylessness*' which '*constituted
The reality behind the concept of a... 'proletariat*'', while at
The same time acknowledging '*differences which belie
The homogeneity...the term 'proletariat' connotes*'; according
To Lockwood, R. Hilferding's 1927 study of monopolistic
Capitalism, *Das Finanzkapital*, elaborated on Weberian lines:
'*The increasing impoverishment, insecurity, and caste-like
Character of the propertyless class would override internal
Differences and provide the principal dynamic of the class
System of late capitalism. And into this vortex of '
Proletarianisation' the blackcoated workers were to be*

Irresistibly drawn' – but, this projection reckoned without
Knowledge of future socio-economic settlements:
*'The diversification of the occupational structure and...
Excursion of the State into'* provision of welfare *'have
Rendered obsolete the idea of a... solidary proletarian class
Consciousness'*; as to other differences which separated
Statuses or perceptions of statuses, blackcoated workers'
'Greater degree of job-security', though *'short of the full
Independence which comes with property'*, was *'a partial
Alternative to ownership'*... also to be *'included in a calculus
Of relative rewards'* were *'the non-pecuniary'* perks of office
Work, *'its cleanliness, comfort, tempo, hours, holidays'* which
Emphasised clerkdom as a *'superior type'* of employment –
Crucially: *'To examine the market situation of a group is not
Enough to arrive at the typical... interests of its members,
Because interests are never purely material'* – most blackcoat
Benefits were symbolic; partitions in offices planted mazes
Of stratification, labyrinths of ranks and grades, but
Conditions for manual workers were starker, thus most
Conducive to class consciousness, growing antagonisms,
Alienation, gazed over from above by visible invigilators –
Employers, *'superiors'*, whip-hands – like galley slaves; shop
Stewards, representatives and go-betweens with management,
Corporals of the closed shop floor, negotiators, petitioners,
Interpreters, sometimes co-operators, in themselves could not
Be class-reconcilers; *'The whole atmosphere of the productive
... unit'* germinated *'impersonal antagonism'*, management was
Socially insulated from workers through *'commensal
Conventions of the factory'* as well as *'the dual system of
Facilities for Works and Staff'*; by complete contrast, *'the old
Paternalistic... counting house was... inimical to... common
Identity among clerks'* with its *'absence of any... blockage of
Mobility'*; the credentials and incentives of clerkdom were
More abstract than material, such *'middle-class values are...
Much less acceptable to the more class-conscious elements of
The landed aristocracy and working class... This
'Bourgeoisification'* ('embourgeoisement' in more modern
Sociological parlance) and *'ambiguity'* ratcheted up

Occupational snootiness; the magnified *'status consciousness Of the blackcoated worker was produced by his marginal Social position, and by the vicious circle of clerical 'Snobbishness' and working-class 'contempt' to which it gave Rise'*; by Lockwood's time of writing, the late Fifties: *'brain Work" was 'less and less the hallmark of middle-class status'* ... As an aside, Geiger of Mass Observation stated in 1949: ' *'We may observe... all those who live by the sale of Their labour power. We attempt, on the basis of Mass Observation, to gain a picture of how they feel, think, react And behave on average"* – oxymoronic to some, *'blackcoated Unionism'* was, at length, grown from a soil of multi-grained Nourishing, but while this facilitated collective action, mutual Aid, and collective bargaining, it didn't smoothly morph into Class consciousness – a more thorough universal perspective Which also encompassed other types of employees; hitherto Less threatening *'friendly societies'* mutated into *'unions'* More militant in approaches to industrial disputes, by way Of collective bargaining, pickets and strikes, and often Identification with or affiliation to the Labour Movement; Unionisation of blackcoated workers accrued simultaneous to *'Bureaucratisation'* of the office workplace, itself displacing The cosier and more personal managerial paternalism Of the old order of smaller burrows and warrens of offices Which, no matter if more intimate and familial permanently Retarded clerk-consciousness; on the other hand, Bureaucratisation, a subsidiary of nationalisation, stamped Out the old boy networks of nepotism – thus were both, in The phrase of Gunnar Myrdal in his *An American Dilemma* (1944) *'mutually cumulative'*; but though nationalisation had Extinguished nepotism, it was soon to spawn a hierarchical System of grades and ranks streamlined across an industry, Which ruthlessly put aside personal relations and individual Talents as implicit pathways to promotions; post-1920... Only In local government were aspects of the old particularism and *'Cockpit of local politics'* atmosphere retained; by 1939 NALGO membership had quadrupled in fourteen years; but The major clerical union was the Clerical and Administrative

Workers' Union which, with around a million members, had
A mountain to climb in nurturing a common cause among its
Members, *'faced with a huge potential membership which had
Next to nothing in common, except that all of them were
'Clerks', and even that was a highly ambiguous common
Denominator'*; bureaucratisation of banks did not in turn
Result comprehensively overturning the particularism of old
Counting-houses, mobility among bank clerks more buoyant
Than among clerks of other industries – but bank officers
Were blinded to the *'universality'* of their fates by
The partitioning of their industry into private branches;
A *'necessary homogenousness'* was lacking from the banking
Industry for it to be conducive to collective action, perhaps
Something symbiotic in that the bank clerk worked to
The same implicit profit motive of his bank; there was
Special kudos and mystique associated with clerks of big
Corporations, something which never graced the rest
Of their occupational species, they were seen as omnipresent
Olympians of their profession, even by relatively salubrious
Banking clerks, unseen but often heard of as *'the people who
Occupy great blocks of offices in the City and elsewhere or...
Who expend huge sums in... well got-up advertisements in
The Press and on hoardings of the underground... do almost
The same work as the bank clerk... and use the same tools i.e.
A pen and a piece of blotting paper'* – thus the hierarchical
Chain ever high-reaching off into the firmament, all types
Of clerk always looking up to superior positions of other
Types of clerk, like rooks scaling branches; but blackcoats
Didn't always look down on blue collars as a piece in *The
Bank Officer* testified: *'Turn now to the bank clerk who lives
In an industrial area and ask him what he knows about
The great firms... Why, blast furnaces... belching forth flame
And smoke to Heaven... Does he know the men who work
There?... he does, and the women too... They go to work...
Before eight in the morning... their clothes, when not covered
By overalls, are stained and shiny'*; blackcoated snobbery was
Mainly blamed for the difficult birth of clerical unionisation,
But to chroniclers such as Lockwood, this was too simplistic,

And, in any case, in *'factories and workshops'* there was an
Inverted snobbery towards those *'above one's station'*...

VII

Socialists saw blackcoats as *'saboteurs of the Labour
Movement'*, *'Judases for Capitalism'* betraying fellow
Workers for thirty-pieces-of-silver salaries – as opposed to
Dowdier 'wages'– but the reality was nonetheless
That blackcoated workers indulged in *'middle-class
Pretentions on a working-class level of living'* – even back
In the days of the counting-house, black coats and blue collars
Had been neck-and-neck in pecuniary terms; the better
Remunerated clerks were able to acquire a middle-class
Lifestyle, while the best-placed clerks were implicitly middle
Class having had positions secured for them by personal
Recommendation and nepotism (local government was
Notoriously rife with these – a *'cockpit of local politics'*);
In Victorian times some anatomists of class-effects in clerking
Bemoaned the anti-meritocratic old school tie culture
Of recruitment, as Charles Edward Parsons wrote in *Clerks:
Their Position and Advancement*: *'Look... to the youths who,
By the aid of patronage or family influence – the crowning
Curses of clerkship – monopolise... the best appointments to
Which clerks aspire'* yet ungratefully *'saunter homewards,
Weary and languishing, thoroughly convincing the onlooker
... they consider work a horrid bore'*... But *'forming a... more
Numerous body come the young men who (if in many cases
Well read, well mannered... religious) still are not in society,
Place little value on gloves, lunch in the office on bread and
Cheese, clean their own boots, and are not alarmed* [at] *doing
Without a servant... of lighting the fire each morning... of
Never entering a theatre or buying a bottle of wine'* and are
Not too proud for their wives to earn a bob or two darning
Sealskin capes for more well-to-do women; but there were
Some stripes of clerk who regarded their *'social standing'* not

As a *'reward'* in itself but deserving of a reward of *'higher Remuneration'*; as one implausibly named boss – who
Sounded as if he'd surfaced from Edward Upward and
Christopher Isherwood's surreal Mortmere novels, or Evelyn
Waugh's *Vile Bodies* – Benjamin Battleaxe, observed: *'But
How come... if the pay is so miserably insufficient... so many
Seek it; that clerks make their sons clerks... ? Is it not because
Clerks are socially gentlemen* [and] *treated as such? Clerks,
Like officers in the army and navy, or like clergymen, have a
Position as well as a salary'* which is a *'substantial advantage
From the nature of their vassalage... let them consider this as
Part of their remuneration'* (they might have seen themselves
As officers but they were simply corporals of corporations);
Few felt much sympathy for the *'poor, sad snob of a clerk'*;
Hopeless impersonation of one's social superiors was
The unwritten clerkly skill, the lower-middle classes were
Psychical colporteurs of the appetites, tastes and habits
Of the upper-middle classes; this imitation of higher strata
Was pretentious in the extreme, as Lockwood put it:
*'The dress, speech and... mannerisms of clerical
Gentlemanliness were often... exaggerated and perverted'* –
An entire incidental culture of affectation; as was noted in
The Cornhill Magazine in the 1860s: *'It may appear
Paradoxical... the manners of an English gentleman have
More in common with the manners of a labourer than...
A mercantile clerk or... shopkeeper'*; but in the case
Of the lower-middle-class gentleman-aspirant it was of an
Entirely different register, a Pooterish pomposity, speaking
Of oneself in third person, and in mannered language: *'He...
Speaks of proceeding when he means 'going''* as if *'in
The style... of... police reports'*, not for the clerk such luxuries
As *'frankness and forthrightness'*, *'unpretentiousness'* was
'A function of social independence', while *'conditions of his
Work and... orientations of his life... brought... opposite
Qualities of obsequiousness, circumlocution and
Pretentiousness'*; he was *'a gentleman as different from
The aristocratic gentry... above... as from 'Nature's
Gentleman' below'*; clerks *'were drawn from the middle class*

Or... socially aspiring artisan families... Their work was clean
And involved... brain not brawn'; the vague promise
Of advancement '*continued to spur energies and imagination*
In an individualistic direction', one of arrested social self-
Improvement; '*... the faults of the clerk may be traced to*
The artificial atmosphere in which he works and the false
Values which influence his life', he '*might have been*
Propertyless like his fustian-clad fellow in the factory' but '*he*
Was not exposed to the same kind of life experiences', nor was
Ever to experience their '*collective consciousness induced...*
By... machine production and rationalisation' in factories,
Industrial melting-pots for ectopic impulses to mutual
Improvement towards team-thinking spurred on by
The emphatic separation of factory bosses in glass-partitioned
Offices raised up from the shop floor – '*a class distance*' as
R Michels put it, a gap only negotiated by shop stewards,
Portable mediators – or sometimes foremen, shop-floor
Supervisors who occupied a purgatorial position which '*like*
That of the non-commissioned officer, often requires
The incumbent to transmit orders... without fully
Understanding the reason behind the command' and
Subsequently '*in a spirit of undue harshness (e.g. violent*
Swearing)' which '*thus alienates those working under him*'
While he is '*the visible representative of* '*Them up there*''; by
Contrast, offices were more intimate affairs – plenty
Of partitions but no explicit split between office workers and
Bosses, visible boundaries blurred, as with the '*office*' and
The '*works*', and although clerical work was as dully routine-
Oriented, it was of a different rhythm to factory-work; to all
Appearances, offices were uniformed and drably gray, where
'*All jobs look alike at a distance; people sitting at desks...*
Shuffling papers' and because of this '*people acquire symbols*
To distinguish them', thus numerous '*titles*' differentiating
Staff according to tasks – like crows ranked according to
Caws, and nuances of grey and black plumage: jays, magpies,
Hooded crows, choughs, jackdaws, rooks, ravens;
Insignificant badges signalling imagined significance, red
Herrings of interchangeable ranks, bureau crumbs for status-

Hungry white-collar workers, designed to designate *'prestige'* –
All inexpensively, since all salaries were marginally
The same; such tokens bestowed to *'lift the clerk out of
The common rut, stimulate his interest in his job... make for
Healthy competition within the firm... even of the most routine
Positions... Every shorthand-typist would prefer to be called a
Secretary'*; but *'open competition'* transformed the clerk's
Position to a *'cog in a machine'*, part of a *'production-line'*;
Prestige-hunger pangs among uniformed grades partially
Satisfied by office titles, especially important with greater
Commingling of impersonal machines – in order to reduce
Costs of clerical work while making it more productive;
'Mechanisation' was the term of the time, even satirised in a
Poem published in *The Clerk* in 1937: *'Early to bed and early
To rise/ Is really very little good/ Unless you mechanise'* –
But *'office mechanisation'* differed to that of the factory
Where machines were reified to primary importance while
Human operators were treated as appliances – *entfremdung*:
*'Human labour becomes ancillary to the machine instead of
The machine being ancillary to human labour'*; in office
Mechanisation human operators were seen as specialists as
Opposed to mere functionaries: *'Typing is a good example of
This kind of work; the typist is usually specialised in relation
To the machine, but... the tempo of work is her own'* – of all
Machines, the typewriter was the most utilised but least
Mechanised – O how many secretaries sat well-poised at
Typewriters as if perched at pianos; but in some cases office
Workers were subordinated to the tempo of the machine they
Operated, such as *'an automatic duplicating or... 'Hollerith
Machine''* (a primitive computer which summarised
The information stored on punch cards) – *'A state of affairs
Which for Marx and Veblen was the distinguishing
Characteristic of modern factory labour'*, a mechanical
Alienation which could stunt development in some operatives;
But hopes of promotion spiced the office atmosphere with
Aroma of rumours, piquancy of competition, enough to give
Illusion of upward mobility and smoke and mirrors of *'no
Impassable barrier'* – though barriers were invisible;

Mechanisation short-sightedly initiated the creation of *'office 'Factories'*; even tempo-independence of typists was
Compromised in typing pools in larger companies; all these
Factors culminated in what FD Klingender recognised as
The completion of *'the technical proletarianisation of clerical Labour'* – yet clerks still weren't temperamentally proletarian..
JS Harrison noted in *The Social Position and Claims of Book-keepers and Clerks Considered* (1852), clerks were *'for The most part so circumstanced'* their *'absorption into The lower class'* was all but inevitable – there had been
A process of purely material proletarianisation
Of the blackcoated worker, but this he resisted with every
Fibre of his broadcloth – quite apart from what Lockwood
Called the *'blackcoated 'aristocracy''*, those best-placed and
Best-remunerated of the clerkly tribes, the *'mass of ordinary Clerks'*, endured a seemingly perpetual *'penuriousness'*,
Earning around about 34s 6d a week; particularly afflicted
Of the pocket railway clerks ransomed to their stations to
The tune of just 31s a week, who *'lay precariously on The edge of the abyss'*, most starkly after *'rationalisation Of railway administration'*; such was the ubiquity
Of the *'pound-a-week' clerk'* that the National Union
Of Clerks spent much manpower in the pre-war period on
Campaigning for raising the average clerk's wage, to
The princely sum of 35s; but wages were being kept down by
Oversupply of potential employees due to the expansion
Of compulsory elementary education; post-war, the position
Of railway clerks began to improve courtesy of a new
Remuneration deal struck by the Railway Clerks Association;
By the Thirties Depression clerkly salaries were cut and not
Restored until the middle of the decade, but thereafter still
'Lagged behind wages in the quickening recovery'; by
The Fifties, the average salaries of clerks were on the same
Level, if not below, wages of manual workers, though it was
Actual earnings rather than rates of pay that counted
'Especially when the earning capacity has socially observable Effects, such as the income spent on recreation, drinking, Smoking, clothing, etc... little comfort to the clerk... that

The manual worker has to work longer hours for his bulkier
Wage-packet', the '*upward movement of the incomes of*
Unskilled and semi-skilled workmen... proved the most bitter
Pill of all for the blackcoated worker' – his only bonus: purely
Symbolic '*prestige*'... Lockwood could report in 1958 that full
Employment post-1940 and nationalisations post-'45 had,
Through a levelling of earnings between black coats and blue
Collars, resulted not so much in proletarianisation
Of broadcloth as bourgeoisification of the fustian – the lower-
Middle-class hadn't, as predicted, sunk into the '*proletariat*';
But clerkdom had been reformed after the bitter taste
Of unalleviated distress and unemployment of the previous
Hungry decade: '*The depression of the thirties demonstrated*
... the blackcoated worker was not immune from the hazards
Of the market'; Rudolf Hilferding had speculated in *Das*
Finanzkapital, 1927, that the '*possibility of advancement*' had
Been a '*basic factor* [in] ... '*the individualistic outlook of*
The blackcoated worker'; woe betide those clerks '*jettisoned*
On the market', as Leonard Bast in EM Forster's *Howard's End*:
'*Leonard was near the abyss, and at such moments men*
Can see clearly... "I shall never get work now... I have my
Groove, and I've got out of it."'... Lockwood further
Illustrated: '*The goal of the ambitious clerk was a lifelong*
Career of devoted effort... culminating in his eventual
'Indispensability' and ultimate recognition. This was all
Highly precarious', as it was put in an April 1931 issue
Of *The Bank Officer*: '*There is no more helpless figure in*
The ranks of unemployment than the out-of-work clerk.
Paradoxically he is both specialised and unskilled ... In
Seeking new work [clerks] *often have to start at the bottom*
Again or content themselves with temporary employment';
Oppositely, as to the moral price of promotion and mobility:
'*As a man climbs socially, the more his sense of comfort,*
Selfishness and ego is aroused and accentuated... The black
Coat of the... clerk symbolised his middle-class status.
The broadcloth he wore was... only one mark of his distinction
From the working-class man. Running deeper than this
Sartorial claim... was the social gulf'; much was compromised

In the incessant cause of status-seeking, much sacrificed in Order to hang the black coat on the hook of *'respectability'*; *'Among blackcoated workers... status consciousness worked ... to dampen any incipient feeling of identification... they Might have had with the manual worker... his economic Position made him forward-looking, striving... individualistic ... The family from which he originated was middle class, if Not in substance... in spirit'* – the perennial *'shabby-genteel'* ... Now for an intermission with that hoary old music hall tune 'Shabby Genteel', composed and performed by Harry Clifton:

We have heard it asserted a dozen time o'er
That a man may be happy in rags,
That a prince is no more, in his carriage and four,
Than a pauper who tramps on the flags.

As I chance to be neither, I cannot describe
How a prince or a pauper may feel.
I belong to that highly respectable tribe,
Which is known as the Shabby Genteel.

Chorus: Too proud to beg, too honest to steal,
I know what it is to be wanting a meal.
My tatters and rags, I try to conceal,
I'm one of the Shabby Genteel....

There are traces of wear on my elbows and knees,
And my boots have run down at the heels
But it's cruel to criticise matters like these
When a man has grown Shabby Genteel.

VIII

The clerk was *'a willing captive'* of *'the middle-class world'*,
He was defined by what he lacked, such as the necessary
Income and propertied independence to be authentically
Middle class, hence need for an intransigence of aim in social
Climbing, though a glass-intransigence: painfully transparent,
Easily shattered; nothing could disguise his marginality,
Which was his unwitting badge of chagrin, his millstone, his
Albatross: *'He was a marginal man... the frequent accusation
Of 'snobbishness' levelled at the clerk was founded in his
Exaggerated assertion of his middle-classness which in turn
Was a product of his marginality'* (almost like primitive
Witchdoctors who believed that by donning animal skins in
Symbolic ceremonies they could acquire the powers
Of animal spirits, the clerk believed being clad in middle-class
Cloth could somehow transfigure him into something else
With greater, even godlier, gifts); *'The differential in
The reward of blackcoated and manual work... established
In... the counting-house era when literate workers were
Scarce and manual labour plentiful, gave substance to
The... claim of the clerk to a superior social standing'*; but
'Snobbishness' was not only a foible of the lower-middle-
Class clerk, all social stations had sloping platforms and
*'Attitudes of the manual worker reflect an increased
Consciousness of his augmented value and status and its
Obverse – a heightened contempt for the lower non-manual
Worker'*, but they had even less time for those *'above'* them,
As a 1951 special investigation into administrative efficiency
By the National Union of Mineworkers illustrated: *'All
Miners'* and those *'who earn their living by hard work, under
Strict rules, feel... resentful... of those chaps who sit on their
You-know-whats in offices, and push pens... the qualifications
On which* [the clerk] *gets his first job... good appearance...
Address, and manners'* are *'appropriate to a footman or a
Flunkey'*, there had ever been a *'guerrilla warfare between
These two groups'*; in commercial and mercantile clerkdom
'Sons of gentlemen and artisans sat side by side' but were

Sharply separated in promotional prospects; secretaries
Of banks boasted *'as a rule, we should not introduce the son
Of a shopkeeper'* into bank clerking; bank clerks had been
Particularly addicted to maintaining status, at least, up to
The war-torn Forties: *'The conventional necessities of his
Existence... included not only... sartorial and housing
Standards of the suburban salariat, but also... private
Education for his children'*; the bank clerk was affected in his
Machinations towards status but had the affluence to keep it
Up better than most other clerks; post-war the status of bank
Clerks was rapidly demoted to a common perception of them
As affected *'shop assistants'* – this diminished status
Illustrated in social sketches as this from 1954: *'A member of
Staff of one of the Big Five, being hard up... went into a
Workman's café. At his table were two... manual workers.
Our banking colleague pricked up his ears when he heard one
Say to the other... 'Makes me laugh these bank clerks, all
Dressed up in their best clothes and haven't two half-pennies
To rub together!"*... The most important quality for clerks was
'Character', mostly sculpted from the cultic auspices
Of *'work'* – often not work in itself but work as a means
Purely to competitive one-upmanship and profiteering in
Order to end up one's own boss and wealthy enough to be
Able to live out most of one's life in idle leisure; moral
Responsibility was essential, both wealth and poverty
Perceived in very different ways to destabilise individuals'
Senses of responsibility, unemployment always perceived as
More a moral than economic problem, a failing of 'character';
Yet unemployment was something increasingly common and
Impinging for clerical workers whose skills grew less and less
Exchangeable and marketable compared to artisans, while
Only factory operatives and casual labourers were harder hit;
Victorian clerks had by and large circumnavigated poverty,
'Pen-men' were much in demand during the Industrial
Revolution – that *'Awakening giant'* stalking the land – due to
Their ability not simply to be able to read but also to write,
And it was the latter skill on which their perceived *'literacy'*
Hinged, thereby was made their demarcation from the mass

Of other employees, thus were most clerks drawn from
The formally educated middle classes; but post-1870 this
Occupational '*monopoly of literacy was broken down by
The first national provision for the rudiments of reading and
Writing to be taught to the masses of working-class children*';
And with this, certainty of permanent employment started
Diminishing, in spite of greater demand for clerical labour
With the expansion of the service economy, the same year's
Education Act, which brought free schooling to the working
And lower classes, meant, in time, clerical supply soon
Outstripped demand, more and more children of the lower-
Middle and '*Respectable*' working classes attracted to office
Work because of '*the light labour and continuous employment
Not to speak of that broadcloth gentility*', most were sons
Of skilled manual workers, the '*brightest*' of the '*elementary
Schools*' – since the inception of compulsory elementary
Education every '*literate person became a potential clerk,
Thus breaking the hitherto monopolistic position of
The blackcoated worker*'; such oversupply of potential '*pen-
Men*' led to the common derisory aphorism, '*Any fool can be
A clerk*'; by the turn of the twentieth century Britain had an
Epidemic of clerks and not enough situations in which to
Place them, a parlous state of affairs confronted by Sir
George Kekewich in 1909 who blamed '*the overstocking of
The market*' due to '*that national system of education... we
Are so abominably proud of... turning out a nation of clerks*';
Since, as Lockwood noted, '*the pronounced social superiority
Of the literate over the illiterate was... at an end, and what
Had previously been exceptional had now become...
Commonplace*'; additionally, supply was pumped up by
Unscrupulous employers' exploitation of commercial
Apprenticeships either poorly paid or unpaid, unprotected by
The bargaining position of trades and craft apprenticeships:
And mechanisation begat amalgamation and rationalisation;
Clerical labour also faced increased divisions, by gender and
By surfacing of new secretarial skills, typing and shorthand,
Which led to pools of specialisation patchworked in
Partitions, '*a complex hierarchy of departments and offices-*

Within-offices', and ever '*finer splintering of clerical work-Groups*', typing pools of isolated operatives; by the mid-
Twentieth century, clerkdom was no more the exclusive
Reserve of men but saw a new commingling with women –
Now '*blackcoated*' were joined by '*white-bloused*' workers;
A logical extension of the well-worn stigma attached to male
Clerkdom, that pen-pushing office work was generally
'*Unmanly*' – as SF Bullock's eponymous clerk in *Robert Thorne: London Clerk* put it: '*We're a small breed. We aren't*
Real men. We don't do men's work. Pen-drivers... fellows in
Black coats, with inky fingers and shiny seats on
Their trousers... crossing t's and dotting i's all day long'; or,
As the writer of the article 'Shall Our Sons Be Clerks?' in
The Clerk April 1925 opined as to '*this very unmasculine*
Calling', coining the epithet '*Born to be men and condemned*
To be clerks'; another wrote in *The Clerk* of December 1930:
'*The office slave boasts a waist and slender figure, while*
The navvy rolls along, a fully developed man of bone and
Muscle. A young navvy at work is a sight for the gods to envy,
The bowed figure of the young clerk at work must make
The gods weep...'; Mary D Wilson noted in her study
'Vocational Preferences of Secondary Modern School
Children' most boy leavers perceived clerical work as a last
Resort, while manual work was '*the only kind of 'real' work*';
Lockwood noted clerical work which '*carried the stigma of*
Being 'unmasculine' was one of the first middle-class
Occupations to become a feminine preserve of employment',
And so the hoary adage, '*Born a man, died a clerk*' took on
Greater resonance; an emasculated and classless occupation:
Lockwood argued the '*clerk belongs neither to the middle*
Class nor the working class', even within their own ranks
They were stratified – they had a '*status ambiguity*' more
Than any other grouping, made hazier by the blurring
Boundaries between the lower-middle- and upper-working
Classes; there was always '*a good deal of overlap*' between
What Lockwood termed the '*white-collar proletariat*' and
The '*working-class bourgeoisie*', both streams merging to
Form what Karl Marx christened the 'petite *bourgeoisie*' (as

Opposed to the genuine middle class, the *haute*-bourgeoisie);
Hence the reflexive need of blackcoated classes to demarcate
Emphatic distinctions between themselves and those
Immediately below them; this insistence on emphasising
'*Social distance*' was a classic symptom of '*status ambiguity*';
Curiously, it seemed the clerkish class was reproductively
Recessive: according to Richard and Kathleen Titmus in
Parents' Revolt (1942), by the Twenties clerical workers
Emerged '*as the class with the lowest fertility*' – clerical
Sterility; an article 'The Cold Class War' in *New Statesman
And Nation* 1956 noted: '*To succeed occupationally is to
Abdicate from the working class*', to remove oneself from
The '*rank-and-file*' and gravitate to management; in a letter
Titled 'Bank Clerk Lucky Jim' in the same magazine
Of the same year, a clerk wrote: '*... none of my relatives went
To a grammar school, they are all working class, all earn
More than I do, and they pity me in my white collar. They all
Tell me I am middle class now, so now I can be a Socialist'...*

IX

Railway and bank clerks, bottom and top ends of the clerical
Hierarchy, had been relatively untouched by unemployment,
Some of the worst affected had been typists; yet according to
A memo submitted to the Royal Commission on
Unemployment Insurance in 1931 by Herbert Elvin: '*Prior to
The war and the immediate post-war period, it was generally
Assumed... office workers could rely on being permanently
Employed, providing they were efficient and their character
Good*' but '*the industrial Depression which started in 1921...
Completely altered this position*'; whole ranks of clerks
Deracinated with little to show for decades of service beyond
The normal period of notice, many never regained permanent
Employment as clerks, some not regaining regular
Employment again; gray-haired blackcoats were particularly
Badly affected since they '*often fell outside the National*

Insurance limit' and thus were ineligible for state support
During times of *'distress'*; *'This uninsured blackcoat
Unemployment persisted in the early Thirties'* – many of these
Men *'joined the Institute of British Executives, or the 'Over-
Forty-fives Association', and some... the Fascist Movement'*
(Always waiting in the wings to sign up the white
Marginalised, and marginally beigeing); according to
A *Spectator* article in 1936, 'Black-Coated Unemployment':
*'Sweated or unemployed clerks... students graduating into
A jobless world, ex-officers who cannot fit into civilian life...
Such men form the backbone of Fascist... movements'*; there
Were copious clerkly recruits, blackcoated blackshirts
Numbered chillingly many; older white-collar workers in
Particular found it almost impossible to find other jobs once
'Out of the careers run in a well-worn groove' – back to
The Leonard Bast bind again; *'the paradox of their situation
As unskilled specialists'* meant *'they... often had to work...
Below their previous status and remuneration'*... Relative
Deprivation was starker for office workers when out of work
Since they could no longer afford to fund affectations, normal
Standards of living, they'd invested in long-term aims for
Themselves and their children's education based on
The assumption their profession was secure and permanent,
While onus was also on them to *'impress'* prospective
Employers with polished appearance, but the only polish they
Could get while unemployed was the off-putting waxy shine
To the coat, and *'badly frayed'* white collar; *'They suffered as
Acutely as almost any other group due to the lack of
Communal provision for their plight and the conventional
Expectations of their position'*; clerkdom had always been
Perceived as a path to higher prospects, and many counting-
House clerks had progressed to mercantile commerce;
*'Particularism played a large role in the career pattern of
The clerk and... chances of success were not always related...
To merit'* and in spite of common perceptions there was much
'Blocked mobility' in clerkdom, more so as amalgamation
Loomed large; in the inter-war years there was promotional
Stagnation, even within clerical grades – nationalisation

Improved the situation temporarily but cherrypicking
Of public school recruits scooped up for upper echelons crept
Back with the return to privatisation... As to out-of-work-
Clerks' increased material distress and its alleviation, little has
Been documented, since most were not inclined to seek
Assistance from private charities, trade unions, Parish Relief,
Means Tests or doles due to their *'natural sensitiveness from
Asking for any assistance'* – as were the lower classes
Of whom it was expected, stigmas notwithstanding; but for
The lower-middle classes fallen on hard times, the *'skidders'*,
There was the added chagrin of having slid down the rungs
Of status to a purgatory of a very private type of poverty
Among immediate relatives, a more cloistered, introspected
Destitution in obscurity, on the same material level as classes
Less educated who would show them no empathy, only
Suspicion of their reserve and bookishness, while their own
Class shunned them – thus was punishment for the lapsed
Middle classes: poverty without prop of fellowship – poverty
At its most spiritually crippling; some such *'skidders'* partial
To outbursts of self-pity, even resentment towards those
Below them whose plights appealed more to public concern
And charity – as a poem in *The Clerk's Journal* expressed it:

*I don't growl at the working man, be his
Virtue strict or morality lax,
He would strike if they gave him my weekly wage,
And they never ask him for income tax.
They take his little ones out to tea in a
Curtained van when the leaves are green.*

*But never flower, field nor fern, in the
Leafy lanes have my children seen.
The case is different, so they say, for I
Am respectable – save the mark!
He works with the sweat of his manly brow
And I with body and brain – poor clerk!*

Poor clerk indeed to not procure by hand *or* brain the full
Fruits of his industry; that poor clerk's precariously rhyming
But sufficiently figurative verse – most satisfactory for its
Polemical purpose and supremely confident in its bread-and-
Jam enjambments – foretasted the full vanilla flavour of
John Davidson's verse-ventriloquism in his clerkly Kipling-
Pastiche ballad 'Thirty Bob A Week' of five years later:

> *I couldn't touch a stop and turn a screw,*
> *And set the blooming world a-work for me,*
> *Like such as cut their teeth – I hope, like you –*
> *On the handle of a skeleton gold key;*
> *I cut mine on a leek, which I eat it every week:*
> *I'm a clerk at thirty bob as you can see...*

O how the humdrum rumbles of such umbrage goes on-and-
Blooming-on way beyond end numbers of one century into
Another... Luckier clerks might have found some domestic
Respite by inhabiting boarding houses in more salubrious
Boroughs of London, or better still leafier suburbs wherefrom
They'd commute, but no Bloomsbury, Bayswater or
Camberwell for most of them, just renting shabby rooms in
Mushroom-sprung urban lodging houses East of Aldgate
Pump, there to be daylight-robbed by money-grubbing
Landladies, hope-sapped by pawnbrokers – like so many
White-collared Raskolnikovs – and broke by having to cough
Up for extra-rentals such as meals, laundry, boot-cleaning;
Their only weekly escape plumbed in gloomy nooks of public
Houses, there to rub shiny shoulders with the great unwashed,
Or partake of singalongs in heaving music halls – concerts
Of common music; as did Davidson in his Grub Street days
Of yellow journalism when he dreamt up Borasic clerks a-
Scheming how to make the trumpeting damp come up tulips:

> *And it's often very cold and very wet,*
> *And my missus stitches towels for a hunks;*
> *And the Pillar'd Halls is half of it to let –*
> *Three rooms about the size of travelling trunks.*

And we cough, my wife and I, to dislocate a sigh,
When the noisy little kids are in their bunks...

Clerks roosted in smokier rookeries of coffee-houses,
Establishments of cheaper beans, sorry sights *'with their shiny*
Coats, frayed collars, shabby cuffs and haggard looks' which
'Betrayed the difficulty in trying to reconcile poverty with
Gentility'... In those same Yellow Nineties Walter Gallichan
Under the penname Geoffrey Mortimer published *The Blight Of*
Respectability – An Anatomy of the Disease and A Theory
Of Curative Treatment (1897), a compendious polemic on
Fin de siècle bourgeois gentility; as its Robert Burtonesque
Title implied, its method was implicitly aetiological, as
Re-emphasised in the chapter 'The Pathology of the Disease'
Which started with some Ciceronian rhetoric: *'Have I not*
Said... 'Were it not for the inherited virus,' the veneering girls
'Might have been decent and wholesome women?' Did I not
Indicate a method of prophylaxis, a... gradual extinction of
The taint?'; there was no universal miracle cure for this
Ailment, no bottled *Tono-Bungay* wonder tonic patented to
Get on prescription to dissipate its creeping symptoms – but
Gallichan did recommend an attitudinal regimen to guard
Against it by psychiatric analogy (not then thought offensive
Fallacy): *'Firmness [is] essential in dealing with certain*
Neuroses... not sentimental... pats on the back' – he refused to
Simply *'sprinkle rose-water over the victims'*; Mortimer's
Pathological approach is at times off-putting to modern
Sensibilities, its period semantics steeped in Lombroson
Symbolism: *'... congenital cases of Respectability are*
The most stubborn, and the prognosis cannot... be... described
As 'good'' – these are, after all, *'the folk who live... without...*
Any cultivation of the æsthetic and poetic sides of
Their natures' made more grotesque by *'a dour religiosity of*
The ultra-puritanic type' all of which is the *'result of 'the ape-*
Like faculty of imitation' in their forbears'; genealogical or
Eugenicist in thrust Gallichan's satirical tone was ambiguous
But buoyed on hyperbole so as to better lance the boil
Of Respectability: *'What were the peculiarities of these*

Ancestors whose idiosyncrasies have degenerated...? They
Tried to be conventional... *no matter to them what Bacon or
Diderot or Herbert Spencer said about... life... They were
Afraid of God, but... more afraid of Mrs Grundy'*... How to
Convince the patient they are sick? *'Respectability presents*
[As] *most neurotic diseases: the patient does not understand...
He is ill'*, and even if he does, *'has no desire to be cured'*; one
May try to shake him from his off-colour complacency with
Violence of rhetoric: *'Scarify him mentally... with Titanic
Laughter at his wretched hallucination. Kick his preposterous
Idol till the sawdust flies out of it;... tear off its flimsy tinsel'*...

X

Mortimer's polemic was composed in exceptionally polished
If pompous prose: *'Respectability, like vulgarity and prudery,
Is an Anglo-Saxon attribute'*, it *'stands for gentility'*, and *'to
Call a decent... man respectable is to dub him genteel'*;
Gallichan's clipped style and curt tone cut from journalistic
Cloth having been among the first clutch of pens at the *Daily
Mail* (supplemental voice of Villadom), a polymath whose
Prolific published output ranged from eugenics to ornithology
– Adept at monographs on nuances of human plumage,
Particularly the suburban species; one might suppose at times
'Mortimer' was Gallichan's attempt at a scathing satirical alter
Ego of Senecan calibre (in tribute to both I alternate
The names); *'The respectable man is a slave to convention...
A stick-i'-the-mire. He is fearful of being deemed a crank, so...
Succeeds in becoming a nonentity... Grundy, Bowdler, and
Podsnap'* were his three *'shoddy' 'gods'*; Mortimer waxed
Aphorismic raptures poeticising contempt for *'Respectability'*:
*'The very word... leaves a bad flavour of middle-class hashes
In the mouth... wafts to the nostrils the reek of stuffy parlours
With horsehair couches, dried grass, and wax flowers'*; its
Personification, a *'factory-made cheap line in humanity, with
A few prim... superstitions, no reasoned morals,'* who on

Sundays troops his brood *'to hear Boanerges hold forth at The tin Bethel at the end of the street'*; Gallichan's exquisite Sketches on *'Respectable'* etiquette and its strained adherents Were bourgeois equivalents to *Mayhew's Characters'* lumpen-Proletarian depictions: *'Another sort... lives at... Clapham... His daughters spend... their time... blocking the pavement in Front of drapers' shops... Mamma and the girls... gangrened With Respectability... are simply mechanical dolls. Says a Woman concerning these types: 'I have known miners, Railway men... wool workers... who have denied themselves Physical necessities to buy and read a book, attend lectures, Or a concert. I never knew a middle-class woman guilty of Such a glaring want of common-sense"*... Gallichan relayed The anecdote of *'a woman... horribly crushed in the Crewe Railway accident'* who *'begged the surgeon with her dying Breath to set her bonnet straight. It was not death... she Feared, but... that grimmer monster Respectability'*; Mortimer's polemic gathered pace in its Mongol-like sweep: *'No fanatical fakir ever endured the torments that some English folk inflict upon themselves before the Mumbo Jumbo Of Respectability... Not content with warping our national Character... we have corrupted decent barbarians by Inoculating them with our miserable disease'*, illustrating our *'Superior'* prudishness: the young *'Hos'* and *'Moonah'* maidens Encountered by Élisée Reclus in his *Primitive Folk* were Groomed to be as *'Respectable as the female natives of Stoke Newington'*: the *'damsels of the Curumbas tribe wore aprons Of leaves suspended from a bead waistband'* but the *'British Matrons thought... such scanty drapery... abominable'* so Instructed *'four corporals... of infantry'* to *'drag the leaf Aprons from* [them]*'* and *'put the women in... petticoats... What a glorious triumph of Respectability... this compulsory Clothing of innocent... women by Tommy Atkins and his 'pals"* – As with the best rhetoricians, Gallichan spouted potent Aphorisms to add figurative weight to his polemic: *"Decent Society' is full of these whited sepulchres'* – our culture is *'Corrupted by the mephitic blight of Respectability'*; Gallichan's galloping campaign grew more progressive:

'When Darwin told people... their early progenitors were
Hairy and ape-like, with prehensile feet, great canine teeth,
And tails... Respectables jeered at him, and said... they were
'Only a little lower than the angels,' and that monkeys must
Have been fashioned as travesties of men. But though we have
Moved upwards' as primates *'man still exhibits'* primitive
Instincts of *'race prejudice, patriotic bias and... class'* – eight
Years later TWH Crosland wrote in *The Suburbans*: *'Man*
Was born a little below the angels, and has been descending
Into suburbanism ever since'... Mortimer continued:
'The proletarian of the sixteenth century could not read nor
Write; but... was probably less vulgar than... his descendants
Whose acquaintance with... literature is restricted to
The gutter library of... snips and racing tips'; Gallichan
Gushed nostalgically for the once reclusive vogue among
Creative geniuses when *'the philosopher and... man of*
Letters... was separate from... the crowd... partly owing to his
Bohemianism... None... qualified themselves for lionisation in
Society' – such misanthropic splendour in contrast to
The decadence and superficialities of Gallichan's Yellow
Nineties where *'the philosopher has been lured from his den;*
The poets have come down from Parnassus to sport with
The nymphs of Philistia... and the recusant and... pariah sat
Down to table with... dignitaries of... Church and State',
Concessions *'not without their perils for... philosopher and...*
Artist... that comes of being au fait *in... frothy small talk of*
Drawing-rooms'; Mortimer had admirable disdain for
Networkers and hacks of cultural life, fingers-on-the-pulse
Opportunistic Jasper Milvains who blighted lives and artistic
Causes of idealistic, deracinated Edwin Reardons – polar
Opposites of the pen in Gissing's *New Grub Street*: *'An author*
Of mediocre ability, possessing self-assertiveness' and
'Bumptiousness' 'can far outpace the shy genius in the race for
Public esteem', for *'Society closes the door upon the needy*
Philosopher... but... throws its portals wide [for] *the adept of*
Claptrap'; Mortimer praised Benjamin Disraeli as sartorial
Exemplar of the bohemian spirit amidst the Establishment,
Who sometimes attended dinners in *'green velvet trousers...*

Canary-coloured waistcoat' and *'wideawake hat'* – Dandy
Statesman, Beau Brummellesque fop of Parliament, flouter
Of *'the mufti of convention'*... Gallichan blamed Thomas
Carlyle for facilitating the cult of Respectability in cultural
Criticism, who *'jeered at and snubbed his contemporary
Writers;... despised mere literary artists'* and set the tempo for
*'A host of minor essayists, journalists, and literary hangers-
On'*; such cultural reactionism, to Mortimer, had a deleterious
Effect on academies: *'... seats of learning become fusty
Abiding-places of mouldy pedantry'* – then qualified himself:
'I am not tilting at universities', but he was pointing out that
They had *'degenerated from halls of knowledge into mere
Forcing beds... of Respectability'* – Gallichan took particular
Aim at marketisation of ancient spires: *'Plutocracy has taken
The colleges... Knowledge has been cramped to suit
The whims of millionaire patrons... big capitalists'*; Mortimer
Cited Grant White's study *England Within and Without*: *'He
Tells us... the British philistine is 'perfect of his kind', that
'Philistinism pervades the whole... of Great Britain South of
The Tweed"*; Mortimer, naturalist and metaphorically pith-
Helmed explorer of deepest suburbia, having observed
Respectables at close quarters as natives of Villadom in
Their natural habitat, turned to closer inspection of the upper
And lower classes: *'... civilised people... lead barbaric lives'*:
In *'the highest class... as in the lower circles, we find...
Animalism graven on patrician faces, and proclaimed in
The... smoking-room, and... covert-side... all our peers are not
Ultra-barbarians; neither are all our bargees and
Coalheavers savages'* but the *'tone'* is *'as low... in the mansion
As in the tenement'*; Mortimer impeached capitalism as
Barbaric: *'Millions toil'* so that *'a coterie of hereditary Lords
And titled parvenus'* can *'enjoy... leisure which they mainly
Devote to... the killing of time'* – mass Stockholm Syndrome
Of citizenship under capitalism, subjecthood under Monarchy,
Psychically ransomed for crumbs of consumerism, *panem et
Cercenses*, spawning British exceptionalism, rampant
Patriotism peaking at height of Empire: *'It is the boast of
The... patriotic Briton that he lives in a highly civilised*

Country... that climate, or insularity of position on the... globe
... have... made England the foremost nation on Earth', this is
The dogma of the *'latter-day Anglo-Saxon, who thinks without*
Thought' – what today some might term 'Gammonism'; *'When*
We ask for an explanation of the term Civilisation, we usually
Hear an enumeration of... material products, money, and
Gatling guns' – we must *'question whether a Society that*
Grants titles to its... money-grabbers is clean-purged of its
Antique barbarism'; Gallichan was sceptical of all honours,
Canny as to how academising of minds could lead to
Complacencies of scholarship: *'Such award... narrows and*
Mars... thinkers who are elevated to a throne of authority',
Even if these *'laureates' 'pipe an undernote of revolt in*
The sequestered grove' at the *'sting of... vulgar rank'* –
The grasping after Respectability seemed to Gallichan
Peculiarly middle class, preoccupied with appearances,
Chronic dissatisfaction with one's place, unappeasable
Aspiration, lacking the present-ness of the upper and lower
Classes, as pleasure-seeking as these but not as frequently
Pleasure-securing – but he was as scathing towards classes
Above and below them, all classes covertly coveting lives
Of idleness: *'... not the leisure to refine the mind, but... to vie*
With the... upper class in dissipation... a barbaric aim of life
In all classes... We are rich and luxurious... far above
The savage. Yet how far? Our leisured and affluent have...
Returned to... employment of a pre-pastoral epoch. Truer
Barbarians never existed' than *'those whose whole thought,*
Energy, and wealth are given up to sport' – the spiritual
Philistinism of public schools; produced such *'rude types... with*
Their... strange drawling... caddish hauteur... rampant
John Bullisms... innate aversion to thought and earnestness';
Gallichan continued satirically: *'If... men and women of...*
Broad sympathies go... into Barbaria and Philistia as apostles
... of light' they must be prepared for not being *'beloved of our*
Children of darkness in Belgravia and Bloomsbury'...
Mortimer praised that part of the proletariat that had fought
Against circumstance to improve themselves in spite of *'lack*
Of advantage in the past, and... scant opportunity in

The present' – the 1890s saw a ripening of anxious corporals;
*'It is a great thing, this educational advance of the tool-
Skilled'* set against the otherwise dismal backdrop of *'English
Epicurism'* which *'is mostly of the lower kind in every rank'* as
'We apotheosise John Barleycorn with Shakspere'; Gallichan
Was more despairing when it came to those whom Marx had
Lumped together pejoratively as lumpenproletariat: *'More
Pitiful... the... untameable of the slums... philanthropy can
Merely patch a rotten vestment'*; being phrenological again,
Mortimer presaged Beveridgian gradualism not entirely
Guiltless of eugenics-inflected thinking, respectable stigma
Of Social Hygienism: *'We are learning... congenital crime is
A subject for the physiologist and... mental pathologist. So,
Too, with the plague of chronic destitution... Instinctive
Barbaric pity urges liberal almsgiving; but... sympathy
Needs... control in its gratification as purely animal appetites
... We should... destroy the sources of hopeless want, as we...
Exterminate disease microbes in the body'*... Building to his
Triumphant summing up, Mortimer strutted about his
Sentences like a cocksure prosecutor addressing the jury
Of his readers tasked to decide a verdict on themselves:
*'I have endeavoured to convince you... Respectability is anti-
Social, improgressive... The world's greatest moral worthies
Have been the Non-Respectables... Unconventionalists...
Eccentrics... We must pull down that Idol Respectability from
Its throne'* which *'does not mean... we are to become ruthless
Vandals'* but *'integrity of character can have no alliance with
Intellectual insincerity and social hypocrisy. We need more
Brave-hearted... heterodox thinkers'* – Respectability's
*'Ravages... will... destroy our prestige, and we shall fall as
Babylon, Rome, and Greece... Our social affections are
Blighted... our emotions... shrivelled, our national virility
Enfeebled'* by this *'insidious virus... sapping our vitals... I
Leave it to Anarchists, Socialists... and the rest to settle
Whether the shoddy God, Respectability, is to reign
Despotically over England'*... Respectability's blight would
Stay and mutate throughout the twentieth century up to
Lockwood's time of writing, the late Fifties, and ultimately

Mutate into its ultra-individualistic, hyper-philistine
Apotheosis with the return to selective 'Victorian values'
Of Thatcherism that made 'greed' 'respectable' again; such
Abstracts as Respectability mattered almost more to aspiring
Lower-middle-class clerks than material concerns; invisible
Privileges on which gentlemen's agreements hinged had auras
All their own and *'enabled them to claim middle class status
In spite of... income'*, their values, mores and aspirations
Separated them from the working class but their incomes
Distanced them from the middle class, so they became
Middle-class imitators on working-class pay, part
Of a *'salariat'* whose salaries were as much abstract as actual,
Paid in non-convertible currencies of *'Respectability'*, pennies
Of *'prestige'*, glass-advantages of gratifying vassalages, but in
Pecuniary terms same levels as a wage, a relative but
Respectable poverty, one with its own special appetites and
Tastes particularly acquired to never be satisfied – a Tantalus-
Class; modest remunerations for such time-consuming
Monotonous routines led to temptations to take pecuniary
Short cuts to top up parlous incomes, but for those who
Succumbed punishment was permanent: *'The guilty man,
Without references and with a reputation in ruins, might
Quickly sink into the abyss'* having *"skidded' from genteel
Positions'* into *'last-resort casual occupations'*; RH
Mottram wrote that checking and counter-checking the paper
Trail of accounting anomalies committed by an ex-employee
Banished for embezzlement left him *'acutely aware of
"The curious personal... reflection upon us all"* – reflecting
On how suited to this work his ex-colleague had been, how
Eminently promotable, how *'average'* he was, *'seemed to
Make an abyss yawn beneath all our feet'*; no matter how
Satisfactorily placed the blackcoated worker, he was only one
Lapse in duplicated paperwork from social outcast;
Blackcoated workers were class-commuters, day-travellers
Between social stations, attempting escape from positions,
Prone to mint-ruminations and dreams of breaking free from
Suffocating routines like so many bowler-hatted absentee

Mr. Benns, or umbrella-rolled Reginald Iolanthe Perrins...

{Self-improvement used to be a pastime of the proles –
O whatever happened to all those anxious corporals?}

XI

Richard Church, self-taught writer, poet, noted the *'moral*
Quietism' of his lower-middle-class parents, friends and
Relations during his upbringing, how his sheepish father
Persuaded him to become a clerk like him instead of attending
An art college as the talented son wished – all to appease his
Father's horror at anything unfamiliar, daring, clever-clever,
'Talented', artistic (such peccadilloes of aspiration always to
Be strictly confined to private pastimes and hobbies, but never
Extrapolated into actual occupations); most of all Church
Reflected half-nostalgic/half-horrified at the stultifying,
Stuffy, listless, tea-saturated intimacy and smothering,
hundery, *'hugger-mugger home atmosphere'* of the lower-
Middle class from which he protractedly extricated himself in
Gradual stages like a caterpillar through pupa to wings – yet
His past stayed with him and most of his future writings
Hinged on intrigues towards strained gentility of his
Claustrophobic upbringing which plagued his imagination as
Habit-forming obsession: how integral the *'appearance'*
Of respectability was to his status-anxious parents
Symbolising to them the *'small margin of safety'* which they
'Struggled to maintain between their respectable little home
And the hungry ocean of violence whose thunder never left
Our ears' – for such lower-middle-class families often lived in
Close proximity to working-class folk, albeit flimsily
Partitioned by pretentions and deferred gratification, served as
Continual reminders of what they could become (or whom
They'd be among) should they drop down a rung – but
The lower-middle class took little consolation in looking
Upwards to where they presumed they wanted to be, such

Heights of superior confidence made them dizzy – a class-
Vertigo at reaching such a high *'altitude of living'* as Jack
London's Martin Eden deemed it among the educated... In
The army, of course, confidence was key to securing a
A commission, though plenty opted for lower key non-
Commissioned posts, corporals, lance corporals, or the ranks
To concentrate on some paper self-improvement, and those on
The cusp of social self-improvement, the upper-working and
Lower-middle classes developed appetites for grasping,
Prehensile social climbers up proverbial ladders – who when
In the army had shown keenness to *'get on'* and an appetite
For stripes, upwardly mobile, sometimes a bit snobbish, but
Above all terrified of tipping back into the black abyss
Of unabashed hardship in slummy origins – for there was
Such a dreadful thing as downward mobility, *'skidding'* down
The ladder – desperately trying to spring free from shadows'
Grips, hungry to hop up lower rungs – Hungarian-born British
Serviceman and Left Book Club author, Arthur Koestler,
Coined an epithet for these serge self-improvers, *'Thoughtful
Corporals'* who inhabited a figurative *'Thoughtful Corporal
Belt'*, or *'Anxious Corporals'* as the phrase became – and
Certainly their thirst for intellectual sustenance was not only
A symptom of curiosity but also a kind of anxiety, that kind
That frets at the clock when trying to soak up knowledge,
Particularly during wartime when the mind might be
Destroyed at any minute; a kind of anxiety that hankers after
Intellectual certainties for a sense of existential security –
Khaki Kierkegaards; craves information as if to satisfy some
Vitamin deficiency of the mind, educational anaemia; as
Prolific writer and chronicler of the working class, Richard
Hoggart, author most notably of *The Uses of Literacy –
Aspects of Working Class Life* (first published by Chatto,
1957; taken up by Penguin, 1958, to become a bestselling
Pelican) related when writing of his time in the army: *'We had
A kind of code that if there was a Penguin or Pelican sticking
Out of the back trouser pocket of a battledress, you had
A word with him because it meant he was one of the different
Ones'*; and corporal is, after all the most anxious rank, lowest

Of the non-commissioned officers yet crucial, climacteric
(From the Greek *klimaktēr*, translated literally as *'rung of
A ladder'*, though its more modern meaning is *'critical point'*)
For the occupant with one foot on the lowest rung
Of the ladder, and one boot still on the ground with
The common private, the upper-working-class and lower-
Middle class dovetail military station, neither one thing nor
The other, and the occupant has to carefully negotiate between
The strata either side of them – private and sergeant (while
A lance corporal is effectively a private with a stripe to show
Proto-promotion, more responsibility for no extra pay) –
Sometimes sorely misplaced, as sheltered, bookish, lower-
Middle-class National Service conscript, Lance Bombardier
Evans, anxious to get an officer's commission to lift him out
Of the toxic rankers' mess in John McGrath's 1966 play
Events While Guarding The Bofors Gun... Now we look
Sharp to Koestler's metaphorical *'corporals'* in Civvy Street,
Out of uniforms into muftis, incorporating the lower ranks
Of the middle classes, but particularly the upper-working
Class, skilled trades and blue collars, shop stewards and union
Reps, a working class not only conscious of its insecure place
In the scheme of things, but curious too, conspicuously
Curious to pick up fruits of knowledge that might – apart
From anything else – help them procure more fruits
Of their labour as was siphoned off in profits for the bosses,
Surpluses theirs by right of effort – and if capitalism
Conspired still to keep their pays capped at subsistence so
They could never save a penny, certainly not afford much
Of commodities they themselves produced – these tradesmen
Tantaluses– then at least now there were ripe pickings
Of knowledge offered cheaply on low-hanging *Woolworths*
Branches whose mint contents were worth so much more than
Pennies, intellectual currency... Tattoo-covered Buddhist
ASB Glover was expert editor of the Pelicans, his
Photographic memory had snapped up the entire contents
Of *Encyclopedia Britannica* while serving time in a prison
Whose name escapes documenters; thick and fast the titles
Came: Arthur C Clarke's *Exploration of Space*, Boris Ford's

Pelican Guide To English Literature, Jacquetta Hawkes'
A Land, G.M. Trevelyan's *A Shortened History of England*;
Hoggart's *The Uses of Literacy* became a founding text
Of Cultural Studies, staple for self-improvers, its account
Of a working-class upbringing in Thirties Leeds, and repulsed
Appraisal of popular culture's loss of authenticity under ersatz
Mass-culture of advertising, television, cinema, fashion, pop
Music and consumerism, ensured it was a bestseller among
The discerning for its bite and clout, it absorbed the Angry
Young Men, entranced the Kitchen Sinkers unclouded by
The milkshake-thick, candyfloss and neon-coloured Fifties,
Sold 20,000 copies per year throughout the Sixties; Pelicans
Hopped and skipped in persistent popularity, not upset by new
Trends of Vespas and espresso bars, winklepickers, uppers
And downers, Purple Hearts of the working-class Mod youth
Culture keeping spruced, slick and clean in difficult
Circumstances, souls slaking spirit-lifting up-tempo Tamla
Motown but otherwise aspiring office boys or shop assistants
Of materialistic tastes and principles spiked with Bespoke
Spices, a curious contradiction of psychedelic consumerism
Salted with a hint of the austere – Mods were the crop-topped
New model ergonomic Roundheads, sharp-suited disciples
Of scowling pseudo-discipline, Puritans in pinched Sta Press,
White socks, Italian suits, thin ties, khaki parkas – magpies;
Hoggart's Pelican masterpiece in part worshipped at the feet
Of the Penguin Brief, and for all those who feared that flash
Of Promethean orange flame might fade – it simply
Transposed to gas-blue as Pelicans raised the plateau towards
A new pedagogic peak, Hoggart at the vanguard of a second
Generation, himself a working-class grammar boy and
Graduate of that first revolutionary wave, Pelican disciple...
Hoggart's prose was painterly, his eye for detail and linguistic
Gifts struck so many who read it, multitudes of willing
Students and autodidacts who'd taken similar paths to him,
His crisp descriptions, prose sketches, word-pictures
Of the upper-working and lower-middle classes, Lowryesque,
Made this social document evocative as well as didactic,
Particularly in its focus on objects as descriptors of proletarian

Personalities: *'The half-light lace curtains... establish your*
Privacy; the... doorsteps yellowed with scouring-stone further
Establish... you are a 'decent' family'; depictions pitch-perfect,
Empirical but tempered with semi-academic eye, Hoggart
Knew his subject inside and out, polemical and domestic,
Deeply poetical, terraced-and-lean-to'd urban Leeds his
Concrete Milk Wood: '... *the aspidistra has gone in favour of*
The ragged-country-lad-eating-cherries... or the big-girl-in-a-
Picture-hat-holding-two-Borzois or a single Alsatian. Chain-
Stored modernismus, *all bad veneer and sprayed-on-varnish'*,
An aesthetic revolution, ascendancy of kitsch: *'Replacing*
The old mahogany; multi-coloured plastic... chrome biscuit
Barrels and bird-cages... these things subserve... domestic
Values... The deep window-sills give opportunity... for some
Exterior colour... a box of rank... nasturtiums or... geraniums',
Curtains can't *'be kept 'a good colour' even with frequent*
Washing in Dolly blue or cream... The smoke and soot from...
Nearby factories and railway lines creep in'; Hoggart the guru
Of working-class struggle, gritted gentility, observer of lives
Of *'tightness and contriving'* perpetually *'on relief'* or *"a bit*
Short'... A situation... full employment and [the] *Welfare State'*
Had done *'a great deal to alter, but not as much as might be*
Thought; ... old habits persist' – hardship's stubborn stains;
The hard-pressed housewife managing on what meagre
Amounts the 'Guardians' would begrudgingly give, mostly in
'Coupons exchangeable at specified grocers', she'd *'helped*
Herself along by smoking Woodbines – furtively, in case
'They' found out', the Guardians again, and many a son was
'Trained to put the twopenny packet in the drawer without
A word if he came back from the shop to find a visitor home' –
Guardians were poverty's paternalistic lamp-pointing Gestapo;
The care-wrung mothers who pinched themselves, that is,
Deprived themselves of any expense, went without so kids
Could be clothed and fed, perhaps a bit of pin-money once
A month, should have popped a *'pessary'* in all those years
Ago, scrimping and scraping, doing a spot of charring to
Supplement the pension if God forbid something happened to
Her whippet-husband chained in the prong of underpaid

Employment, and if he lost his position he'd still need his little
Luxuries to keep hold of some morsel of self-respect: '*If he is
On the dole... whether... through ill health... ill luck or
Shiftlessness... Self-respect is involved; 'A man can't be
Without money in 'is pocket'; he would then... feel 'tied to' his
Wife*', prisoner of apron-strings, so must still be permitted
Pennies for his baccy and beer plus occasional flutters;
'*Fifteen cheap cigarettes a day... for a man... drawing
The dole... Such things as cigarettes... it is felt, are part of
Life; without them, life would not be life*' – puff-crutches for
Coping; whist-drives for housewives over thirty-five; boys
Might get some meagre treats '*going to the paper-shop*' for
Their Saturday magazines, 'The Wizard *or* The Hotspur', and
For '*licorice or some cinnamon root from the chemist, two
Pennyworth of broken locust*', and on Sundays pastoral trips
'*With jam-jars to a dirty stream... for sticklebacks*', or
'*Blackberrying... past the church with the whalebone arches*' –
Hoggart, a social-documenting Dylan Thomas of Leeds...
Entire working-class communities committed to Calvinistic
Faith of '*thrift and the cult of cleanliness*' – Hoggart could be
Judgemental: '*Among those who... ignore these criteria,
The uninhibited... and carefree spirits are outnumbered by
The slovenly and shiftless whose homes and habits reflect...
Inner lack of grip*'; books were seen as passports to self-
Improvement and thereby mobilised one's social prospects;
Here Hoggart gave glimpse of his book-knowledge – some
Autodidacts and scholarship boys unknowingly wear like cub-
Badges – by quoting from Ancient Egyptian scribe Duauf's
Advice to his son Pepi after entering him into the School
Of Books: '*I have seen him that is beaten: thou art to set thine
Heart on books. I have beheld him that is set free from forced
Labour: behold, nothing surpasseth books*' – the School
Of Soft Books was a ballast against the School of Hard
Knocks; there was among the working class '*visceral hatred
Of debt and credit, they'd pride themselves by owing nothing
... even if owning nothing... except a few sticks of furniture...
They cannot bear the thought of having a debt outstanding*'
And here manifested the down-at-heel religion of '*clinging*';

As for an actual working-class religion, apart from football
Worshipped from stone pews, there was a philosophical
Approach in part metaphysically optimistic, taking existence
As proof of some higher purpose, but beyond that, too much
Navel-gazing was frowned upon as pointless and peripheral to
Their lives, such highfalutin questions on the existence
Of God or an afterlife was for Them Upstairs to bother about,
They'd otherwise take it in their stride – '*There must be some*
Purpose or we wouldn't be 'ere'; they had some belief as
Testified in the '*In Memoriam columns of local newspapers:*
How often an 'After-life' is mentioned', a reward after all
The '*hard work 'here below'... the arrival at an easier*
Happier existence' – Heaven, to them, a much-anticipated
Opportunity to put their feet up – spiritually speaking – and be
Waited on for a change... "*A blessed release*', '*A better*
Existence'... *or 'Gone ahead*" – as if on a charabanc trip; life,
For the proletariat, is a constant trial, if not actual Hell, could
At best be described as purgatorial, so it was hoped, even
Presumed, a hereafter would be a lot softer on their sort, and
Heaven could be negotiated along the lines of well-wrung
Washing lines – since real life's punishment enough; '*Here...*
Their kind have been the lackers', from their point of view
'*Heaven will be... the place for 'straightening out'...*
Comforting... time to sit, to get a good rest... There will be a
Reunion with those who have gone before and... been so much
Missed'; up there everything would be done properly, slap-up,
As it should have been down here, '*hence... emphasis on a*
'Proper' funeral, a 'decent burial'... and... cremation as
'Unnatural", all that strange business with smoke and ashes
Smacked of hocus-pocus Catholicism, they liked to put graves
To faces, have tangible reminders of loved ones passed over
Carved in stone – something implicitly Protestant which left
Behind a spiritual footprint; there was a reverence towards
The '*practical Christianity*' of the Salvation Army, always a
Charitable presence in their communities, a kind of brass band
Heart-on-Sleeve Calvinism; they liked to see Christianity in
Action – nothing was of much use if not in action:
'*Their concern is with morals, not metaphysics*', nuts-and-

Bolts, something applicable for those who must *'get along With others, in groups... on an exchange basis... give and Take'* – their only dogma was that faith must be demonstrable, *"Doing good', 'common decency', 'helping lame dogs'... Life... Is 'rubbing along"* but *'you may have 'Christ's teaching'... at The back of your head'*; they put much stock by *'decent-Heartedness'*, were *'unidealistic'*, *'empirical... confirmed Pragmatists'*; most working-class people aspired to *'the good Life'* they'd invariably describe as *'not simply a matter of 'Putting up with things'* but one with scope for a *'bit extra'*, but This was not *'climbing'*, they'd no *'quarrel with their general Level'* just wanted *'a few frills'* – if not *'the good life'*, then, at Least a good afterlife; pleasure-seeking but hardly hedonism, Simply aspiration to sometimes indulge in luxury, partake Of a bit of temptation: *"A little of what y'fancy does y'good'... There is a note... in English working-class life since the Wife Of Bath, which sounds in Shakespeare's... Mistress Quickly... And in the... music-halls'*, the *Keep Calm And Carry On* spirit, A bit of grit, pluck and chirpiness – as opposed to chippiness – *'It gives yer a laugh at any rate'*, *'Wilfred Pickles' 'salty Repartee"*, George Formby strumming his ukulele (*'Turned Out nice again!'*), old-fashioned fairness, *'neighbourliness'*, *'Looking on the bright side'*, keeping your pecker up...

XII

Working-class values were far nobler than those with which Media and advertising bombarded them, as Hoggart Bemoaned: *'The commercial values... show for its own sake, Conspicuous consumption'*; Hoggart asked gnomically: *'By What means may scepticism and nonconformity be made Tarnished ghosts of themselves? Can... 'aving a good time While y'can' because life is hard open the way to a soft mass-Hedonism? Can the sense of the group be turned into... slick Conformity?'* All this framed as Progress, something against Which Hoggart cautioned: *'The pressures of commercial life...*

Becomes a limitless 'progressivism' of things... 'Time marches
On...' says the thrilled... voice of the film commentator' to
'The roll of drums and... blare of trumpets... 'Let the... world
Run for ever down the ringing grooves of change' cries
The advertising copy-writer' in Tennysonian flourish; *'... new*
Dawns... forward movements (marchings and floods)...
The ideas... received tags ('They say it's all relative
Nowadays'; 'They say it's all a matter of your glands')'; how
Uncannily the late Fifties prefigured the Eighties in Hoggart's
Warnings: *'... those ideas, misused, are... tempting a...*
Materially emancipated working-class to have a largely
Material outlook' – what other function did advertising serve
But to tempt? The Devil's in the detail of capitalism's small
Print; *'The temptations... as they appear in mass-publications,*
Are towards a gratification of the self and... a 'hedonistic-
Group-individualism'' – something which would come to
Fruition through Thatcher's tempting of working-class council
House tenants into home ownership through Right-To-Buy
Schemes, blue collar Labourites converted to self-serving
Conservatism only twenty years on from Hoggart's time
Of writing and scrying... Present danger for Hoggart was a
Seemingly more progressive sieving of values towards
Modernised and standardised modes of living: *'Contemporary*
Society has developed... techniques of mutual indulgence and
Satisfied 'ordinariness'' – the resistible rise of mediocrity; *'So*
The popularisers with their... new machines for persuasion
Occupied the open country left', here Hoggart stood as a
Jeremiah warning his own class that more time and disposable
Income wasn't necessarily destined to be well spent, time
Itself was disposable and once used up couldn't be replaced,
Unlike income, and a fat lot of use more time and income if
Almost all attractions were meretricious: *'... mass-production*
Has brought good' but *'the mass-produced bad makes it*
Harder for the good to be recognised. 'Brute necessities'...
Have been greatly lessened. Working-people... have
The freedom of a Vast Vanity Fair for shouting indulgences',
So Hoggart guarded against the *'powerful pressure... from*
Advertising copy-writers... to sell to all classes the ramified

Forms of individualism'; surprisingly, given his progressive
Views, Hoggart warned against '*galloping egalitarianism*',
Which held '*psychology has justified the utmost
'Broadmindedness*'', that its proselytisers were captors of a
Common cramp in willpower imposed upon the masses by
Their own supplication, widespread emptiness of moral
Purpose – '*Anything goes*' is related to "*live and let live*'...
*The open mind has become a yawning chasm. Tolerance
Becomes not so much a charitable allowance... as a weakness,
A ceaseless leaking-away of the will-to-decide on matters
Outside the... touchable orbit*' of which the popular motto was
'*Everyone's entitled to his own opinion*' – Hoggart was
Uncompromising in his philosophical opposition to such
Amorphous '*open-mindedness*': '*The tolerance of men who
Have some strength... is... meaningful; the tolerance of those
Whose muscles are flabby and spirits unwilling is simply
A 'don't-hit-me' masquerading as mature agreement*'; Hoggart
Pre-empted perceived permissiveness on the cusp of the next
Decade which would trip in promptly with the 'Profumo
Affair', and the advent of the Pill ('*with cheap contraceptives*'
Sex was now '*easier*' but mass-promiscuity not so prompt:
'*They are not happily amoral savages disporting in some
Slumland... They do not rollick... like citified versions of
The 'apples be ripe' bucolics of TF Powys... In most cases,
Such activity does not seem to be continued after marriage*');
In growing 'progressivism' Hoggart diagnosed fundamental
Philistinism, dumbing down: '*... complex... or taxing literature
Must... be discounted; good writing cannot be popular today*';
There was a snobbery against the highbrow: '*The publication
Of the British Council Report is made a yearly excuse for a
Tirade on the waste of... public money on highbrow exercises
By flabby young men. A case of homosexuality is used as...
Jumping-off ground for an attack on the debased world of
Bohemia... The Arts Council is a 'fiddle' by a lot of 'cissies'
Who despise the amusements of the plain Englishman; and
The BBC is little better*'... The pilots of this philistine path to
Help the proletariat keep in their place whilst oppositely
Thinking they're on their way up were the red top newspapers

Promoting inverted snobbery on behalf of under-educated
Readerships on whose side they pretended to be: *'Hence...
The embattled low-brow tone of many columnists'* or *'low-
Brow snobbery of... wireless programmes'* where
*'The democratic lust for widespread... opinion unites with a...
Slight resentment'* of *'knowledgeable people'*, and when
*'The experts fall out... there arise... what... Gilbert Harding...
Described as 'the elemental odours of the bull-ring and...
Bear-pit''*; also lamentable is a *'levelling-down... among
The popular columnists... back-scratchers for 'the common
Man'... cheer-leaders of the 'damned compact majority'...
The stiff upper lip and a... cheerfulness outstaring
The aesthetic Gorgon'* – ever more gnomic, Hoggart's
Dystopian projections had been adumbrated by Aldous Huxley's
Brave New World published twenty years earlier:

Hoggart. The eyes would register but not connect to the nerves, heart, and the brain; they would connect to a sense of shared pleasure, of pleasure in simply sharing the unifying object, not in the object itself...

Huxley. That's the price we have to pay for stability. You've got to choose between happiness and what people used to call high art. We've sacrificed high art. We have the feelies and the scent organ instead...

*''Progressivism' assists living for the present by disowning
The past; but the present is enjoyed only because... it is...
The latest and not... out-of-date... each new 'present' holds out
An infinite perspective'* of *'Technicolour... all-smelling, all-
Touching, all-tasting TV'* – Huxley's *'feelies'* feeding through
Like a hungry leitmotif; doubtless Hoggart might have been
Partial to a gramme of Soma had it been a real thing, a drug
Of gradualism, a Cosmo cocktail of cognition, an endorphin-
Releasing spiritual gin, mass opium, which gave *'all
The advantages of Christianity and alcohol; none of
Their defects'* (Huxley), so no more hangovers with pangs
Of agnosticism... Hoggart wouldn't let the issue go, noting

How ironically old school such notions of progress were:
'... the concept of unlimited... progress survives with
The popular publicist' who is *'still of the environment of*
The 1851 Exhibition. To be progressive, 'forward-looking',
'As modern as tomorrow', is still one of the desirable ends-in-
Themselves" – Hoggart's Crystal Palace Paradox, anticipating
The Mods soon to step out in sharp-cut suits, cropped
Haircuts, peacock-strutting bright young gamins with a love
Of jazz, scooters and coffee bars, cue Blitz Baby and his ex-
Girlfriend Crêpe Suzette in Colin MacInnes' pop-culture pot-
Boiler, *Absolute Beginners* (1958); *'This... pattern of*
Assumptions [is] *reinforced, among working-class people... by*
The fact... they are... without a sense of the past', have *'little*
Idea of an historical... pattern' – each generation, beginners
Indeed; *'To be old-fashioned is to be condemned'* except for
'Willow-pattern' mothers – quoting de Tocqueville:
'Democratic nations care... little for what has been, but... are
Haunted by... what will be', copywriters must scoop good
Times coming – that quotable cat also purred: *'Aristocratic*
Nations are apt to narrow the scope of human perfectibility;
Democratic nations to expand it beyond compass'... Hoggart
Saw in *'galloping egalitarianism'* a threat to cultural raising
Of standards, something to stymie meritocracy, dumb down,
Reduce everything to lowest common denominators:
"Anything goes'... can be a verbal posture inspired by fear.
Indifferentism is likely to follow... If all are of equal value,
Nothing is of much worth. There is in the end an emptiness...
The refusal to admit any exceptionableness'; Hoggart inclined
Towards a Nietzschean-Eliotic depiction of the common man,
A hollow man, a moral Cro-Magnon, a Gammon Man,
A brylecreemed empty vessel; Ortega y Gaset's conviction:
'We... need 'a change of heart" – O that Audenic cri de cœur;
'In the age of... public-address systems, the 'common man'... is
For ever hearing... the plummily explanatory tone...
Constantly over-coax, over-sell... 'Do you suffer from – ?'...
'What would you have done?"; the clamour of influencers on
Besieged ears of *'mass man'* became so cacophonic as to
Induce a cognitive dissonance so overwhelming its effects led

To symptoms not unlike schizophrenia – emotional blunting,
Spiritual numbness, psychical palsy, (political) apathy,
(Cultural) catatonia, ubiquitous auditory bombardments, many
And varied intrusive voices of advertising and television:
*'... he is so bespattered by the ceaseless exoteric voices... to
Feel this... to react to this, to do that, to believe this – that...
He... goes dead to it all... develops... a thick... skin for not
Taking notice'* – deaf ears of indifferentism which filter out all
Conflict of narrative, rhetoric and opinion, only a residue
Of cynicism left over, scepticism that might be healthy, if not
Inhibiting, were it not to seep into paranoia: *'It's all
Propaganda in the papers'* – yet still they'll lap up the scraps,
Swear by much of it as Gospel... Employment, as opposed to
Purer occupation, comprises some corruption, *'Honesty is
The best policy'* seems a phrase as quaint as *'the poker-work in
Which it was traced over the brass-bedstead'*; we eternally
Return to the Nietzschean-Eliotic Hollow Man: *'He puts up so
Powerful a silent resistance... it can threaten to become a
Spiritual death, a creeping paralysis of the moral will'* –
The modern disease of disinterestedness, epidemic of moral
Complacency: *'A generation expert at... explaining-away,
Insulated from thinking... suspicious of anything not in itself
Disillusioned or... self-seeking'*; by the Fifties, Eliot's
Psychical Waste Land had come to pass but in an unexpected
Way, not in stones and thorns and scrub and shrapnel but in
Cocktail parasols, milkshakes, candyfloss and formica: *'All
These attitudes... spread a nerve-killing effect... a contracting-
Out'*; anyone who nursed pretensions as to improving things
Or themselves was suspect: *'Ideals may be a sign of lack of
Self-seeking, but they are unworkable... anyone... trying to
'Live by principle'... may be a fool or a prig; look for the clay
Feet'* – if not a fool or a prig then *'probably a hypocrite'*, such
Attitudes, or anti-attitudes, distilled into nihilism:
'The 'Orlick'... and... 'Sweeney' spirit', hence prevalence
Of the spiv who had an equivalent in the lower-middle classes
As Hoggart colourfully sketched: *'... such a man... leans to a
Sporting... gentleman-about-town, effect... a gallant artillery
Captain in mufti, or... a character from... Somerset Maugham.*

He tries to engage the barmaid in sophisticated conversation',
Strives to be visibly *'brisk'*, has *'a dark thin pencil line'*
Moustache, *'His ready smile does not quite reach the eyes...
He carries on conversation in spurts... punctuated by hearty
Laughs... nods, winks, innuendos... jargon of the minor
Commercial world'*, the pub Saloon bar's *'doggy communion'*
The closest he gets to *'a sense of a group'* among *'barrow-
Boys, door-to-door salesmen, and... more prosperous ones
With... a fine brilliantine bloom on their ears, a faint smell of
Perfume'*; Hoggart surveyed cultural cynicism across classes
Noting *'connexions between the 'I couldn't care less' of
The rankers'* and the *"anything goes' of the bright young
Things'... enjoyment in the game of... 'knowingness', in
Blowing the froth off... intellectual small beer, in the Swedish
Drill... of a well-informed... mind'* and *'a fear of emotion
Disguising itself as a rejection of sentimentality'* – all this,
Enervating of the spirit, whittling it down to mere residual
Consciousness: *'Riddled by a fuzzy... egalitarianism...
Believing nothing... we stand on nothing and so can stand for
Nothing'*, in this empty space of human development,
Cynicism and criticism, easy-reflex aftershaves of aesthetes:
*"The teachers have read Lytton Strachey, and the children's
Teeth are set on edge', said TS Eliot. So are the teeth of
The teachers... But there can also be an astringent pleasure
In the condition... There is some amusement... in calling
Continually'* – quoting from Auden's *The Age of Anxiety:
A Baroque Eclogue* (1947) – *'Your lie is showing/Your creed is
Creased'*; Hoggart detected such anti-sentiments in literature
Of the time *'in Hemingway, Maugham, Huxley, Waugh,
PH Newby... Henry Green... Hank Janson... Kingsley Amis...
These writers... differ in... disinterestedness... But all are
Illuminating the same destructive element'* – from *Lord Jim* to
Lucky Jim... Progressivism was about numbers, getting bums
On seats and keeping them there: *'... quantity becomes quality
And we arrive at... monstrous... swirling undifferentiation...
An endless flux of the undistinguished'* where *'every... activity
Is... reduced to a counting of heads'* – surely more to
Democracy than majoritarianism – or *'Koom-Posh-erie'*,

Edward Bulwer-Lytton's idiomatic term from *The Coming Race* (1871) for rule by numbers...? More to popularity than
Simply populism? More to culture than melting down to
The lowest common denominator? This passive receptiveness
To synthetic culture and intellectually-vetted entertainments
Made for grim dystopian predictions from Hoggart's pen:
*'We can soon put ourselves in a position in which we lie back
With our mouths open, whilst we are fed by pipe-line... from a
Bottomless cornucopia manipulated by the anonymous 'Them"* –
Reminiscent of EM Forster's probe into dystopian fiction
In *The Machine Stops* (1909), humans wombed in padded
Electronically connected cells, bathed in artificial air and
Light, skins *'white as a fungus'*, spared pain of personality and
Angst of private thought, a prophetic story, even anticipating
Skyping; by synchronicity, Hoggart echoed Forster: *'So
The claims of conformity increase. 'Only Connect' said
EM Forster, thinking of the conflict... of the inner and... outer life.
'Only Conform', whispers the prevailing wind today. Nothing
Matters... but the majority are probably right... The strongest
Argument against... mass entertainments is not that they
Debase taste... but that they over-excite it... 'enervate' rather
Than 'corrupt'... kill it at the nerve'*... Jeremy Seabrook's *New
Society* reappraisal of *The Uses of Literacy*, almost a Hoggart-
Hagiography, argued the monograph was *'a poem – an elegy'*,
As well as *'protest'* at how *'older working class values were...
Distorted... to accommodate a... disruptive culture of
Commodities... felt as... alien and disturbing'*, the book
*'Reflected all our ambiguous feelings... at... our new social
Mobility'*: as they went to university they found *'thanks to
Hoggart... our social origins had become... a passport to...
Social success... We were entering... 'the caring professions'...
Though we should... have reflected... we were being...
Rewarded for what we saw as our altruism'*; but Hoggart
Had made them well aware of manipulators who had *'tempted
... some of the brighter minds... into a kind of weakening of
Their class – partly for money, partly for... inadequately
Examined reasons'*; greater education made existentialists
Who sought *'to assuage our guilt at... defection'*, they'd

Thought the *'material comfort... being brought to working People'* must be *'unambiguously benign'*, but Hoggart *'was Warning... about a different... impoverishment... these Processes... set in train'* whereby *'living attitudes'* were *'re-Shaped'* to fit *'the consumer economy'*, a *'misshaping of... Relationships, until they became a caricature of themselves'* – How else could it be *'when... selling things to the previously Poor?'* Capital was about to *'turn over... human experience To the marketplace'* hitherto *"protected' by poverty'...*

XIII

Journalism was willing accomplice to this compression
Of cultural parameters, infantilising of information, flat-Packing of facts to fit smallest palates: *'... the popular Press Has to become ever more bitty in its presentation of what is to Be read'* and this was *'gradually ousted by what is only to be Seen. The 'strips' spread like a rash... There has to be some Verbal guidance... all necessary background information... Bubbles out of the characters' mouths'*; forming opinions – Like bubbles – was encouraged, but those opinions were Spoon-fed by red tops to readers until such point they felt so Strongly about so many topics as if the opinions were formed From their personal experiences, opinions not based on Expertise but simply on parroting, opinions imposed by press-Hypnotism: *'... this is an age of 'opinionation'... though few People take the trouble... to understand any problem'*, and this Presumption of personal expertise on all topics no matter how Far outside one's sphere of experience produced compulsive Dependency among tabloid readerships: *'Pleasures of a Constant diet of odd snippets... unrelated scrappy facts, each With its sugary... kernel of 'human interest"*, the red top press Hypocritical as it was hyperbolic with its *'pseudo-moral Janus Glance... used in papers not specially appealing to The working-classes... All have in common the assumption... Their readers are short-winded. All premasticate... material*

So... it shall neither bore nor tax anyone... everything is...
Pepped-up'; magnification was vital to this – Hoggart's
Analogy: '... *mice are photographed from below and*
Their huge shadows passed off as genuine horrors' –
Newspapers and broadcasters in part always acknowledged
Their debt to fiction by referring to news items as '*stories*',
Prose as '*Copy*'; but the tabloids were as adept at abdicating
Responsibility for philistine standards as asserting them;
Popular magazines served to further feed an enervating diet
Of frivolous vanilla information, undemanding titbits, gloss,
Gossip, vicarious thrills: '*They can be accused (as can...*
The thin bonhomie of many television programmes,
The popular film...), not of failing to be highbrow, but of not
Being truly concrete and personal... Popular publicists
Always tell their audience... they need not be ashamed of not
Being highbrow... This is true, but... becomes false
The moment such people say it'; all components of this plastic
Dystopia-in-the-making summed up by Hoggart: '*Most mass-*
Entertainments are... what DH Lawrence described as 'anti-
Life'... full of a corrupt brightness... improper appeals and
Moral evasions' which results in '*passive acceptance*';
Hoggart cautioned: '... *the great majority of us are being*
Merged into one class. We are becoming culturally classless',
But this '*classlessness*' threatened to become homogeneity
Rather than anything emancipating such as that to which
Oscar Wilde aspired in his 1891 monograph *The Soul Of Man*
Under Socialism, a living celebration of individuality over
Individualism, flourishing of full authentic human personality,
Universal rainbow of becoming... Hoggart chided
The knowing complacency of his period: '*There are many*
Who feel... they 'know all the arguments about cultural
Debasement... yet can take it all remarkably easily', there
Seems a '*valuelessness of the permanent open mind*' –
Hoggart's outlook on the transformative power of language to
Grow higher consciousness, encourage human flourishing,
Grew gloomier, merged into Jeremiad: '... *by the end of*
The twentieth century the impact of the written word... will...
Have been a short and almost negligible interlude:... by then

The largely oral and local culture dominant until the latter
Half of the nineteenth century will have been replaced by one
That is again oral, but... also visual and massively public', yet
Still he kept hope in the small but persistent numbers of self-
Improvers, '*people who read because they have an*
Ineradicable feeling that it matters'; he made emphatic
Mention of the '*anxious corporals*' conscripted by
Their consciences and thirsts for knowledge to improve
Themselves, and mutually improve: '*During the last war*
Arthur Koestler wrote... about what he called the 'anxious
Corporals'... the intelligent laymen in uniform. The war mixed
Us all up and the Armed Services, not rich intellectual
Pastures, made such people seek each other out. So some
Highly-educated people discovered... intelligent laymen exist' –
Then Hoggart doubted himself: '*Or is all this a will-o'-the-*
Wisp, a remnant... from years of Workers' Educational
Association and extension-class teaching; or... a romantic
Projection from... those rare but impressive self-educated
Working-men one met... years ago?' – classic autodidacts; so
Now were those anxious corporals becoming stuff of myth,
Figments of nostalgia...? Was it now necessary for language
To re-adapt itself, be less highfalutin and more relatable in
Order to get nobler messages across – not by "*popularisation*'
Or haute vulgarisation', but by being simpler in expression?
Reasons for abstruseness, obscurantism, esoteric coinages
Of language among some cognoscenti symptomatic
Of resistance to communication on a mass scale, an attempt to
Cloister knowledge among coteries, jealously guarded cultural
Capital, even down to personal temptations to solipsism
Among more misanthropic proctors, for '*not everyone wants*
To be friends, to be in touch; and some of those people are
The most intelligent among us'; navigating this new frontier to
Formulating a mass-literature was fraught with dangers, and
Lacking in maps and compasses, for present attempts at
Popular appeal presented their own ironic risks of putting up
New partitions: '*The result is that a close-up intimacy itself...*
Distances us. It becomes an invisible but impenetrable film; it
Separates... writer and... reader from the shock of

The experience being written about'... Even sex appeal
Became streamlined as in the glossiness and passion-
Dampening mirage of glamour, a bugbear of Hoggart's,
The *"cheesecake' presentation'* of *'pin-up photography'* which
*'Used to be... standard decoration for servicemen's billets...
But now... we are all assaulted by them... we are a democracy
Whose working-people are exchanging their birthright for...
Pin-ups'*; so much off-putting ultra-soft pornography
Of curling lips, smouldering stares, arched eyebrows, pluming
Cigarettes, sweat-simulating greased hair; some magazines
Seemed more like comics, pages of *'illustrated jokes... as...
Old-fashioned as an aspidistra'* contrast against *'the new style
Of drawing... derived from the American 'strips' and differing
From the older English ones as a slick milk-bar differs from
An unimproved fish-and-chip shop'*, out on the *'newsagents'
Side-hoardings'* posters of attempts at exotic-looking women
Demonstrably girls next door, just tanned a bit, the *'Arabian
Girl of pleasure'* from 'Law of the Pagan... *homely savagery;
She will have the face and... attractively-waved auburn hair of
The girl who smiles from the fourpenny patterns for knitting
Jumpers'*... To Hoggart this over-baked *junk kultur* eked out to
The working classes was a recipe for inauthentic anti-culture,
A distancing from class experience (class distancing) – so not
Only were workers estranged from their labour but also
Alienated from their leisure: *'Everything has gone vicarious:
This is puff-pastry literature, with nothing inside the pastry'*
But *'a hollow brightness'*; sexuality becomes vicarious,
Voyeuristic, onanistic, pent-up in pin-ups: *'At first they look
Extremely suggestive... Yet... the sex has been machined out of
Them'*, libidos airbrushed out; *'... can one imagine a musky
Body-smell, un-artificially disordered air... on one of these
Neatly-packaged creatures?'*; rhetorical Hoggart felt these
Postcards and posters wouldn't promote *'heterosexual activity'*
As much as *'masturbation: in their symbolic way... promote
That kind of sealed-off sexual response'* – tangentially:
*'The same ersatz quality is... apparent in... 'outspokenness'
Of... the popular press'*, a *'shadow-boxing... punch-pulling,
Harmless muscle-flexing under arc lights... The enemies...*

Men of straw... bogus Aunt Sallies'; Hoggart was particularly
Critical of the journalistic style of contemporary popular
Prose: '*Short-winded sentences... epithets flat and tagging
Dumbly...; the lack of any texture or sense of depth*' (like pin-
Ups!) '*To use writing like this to describe character is like
Building a house from spent matchsticks... This newer writing
Has... a cheap gum-chewing... glibness*' with '*less and less...
Of the fibre of life*' – a prose style for the desensitised: '*We are
In a pallid half-light of the emotions where nothing shocks...
Or sets on edge...; only the constant trickle of tinned milk-
And-water which staves off... pangs of... positive hunger...
Denies satisfactions of a solidly-filling meal*' – junk culture
Of escapist snacking to patch over appetites chronically
Unsated under capitalism; Hoggart found '*the dailies aimed...
At middle-class people*' even '*more unpleasant*' for
Their '*spiritual chauvinism... snobbery, and... cocktail-party
Polish*'; so much working-class reading matter dominated by
Three main categories, each there to titillate thrill-seekers,
Offer escape from mundanity, or satisfy blood-lust:
'*Crime, Science fiction and sex novelettes*' which all had a uniform
Format: '*... flat paper, crude print, vivid glossy cover*';
Detective fiction was especially popular, Raymond Chandler
Distilling Hemingway's curt '*iceberg*' sensibility into a best-
Selling formula, the kind of '*confetti-literature*' Hoggart railed
Against – hack-escapism; Hoggart took a magnifying-glass to
Magazine shops ubiquitous in working-class shopping areas:
'*Their window-space... littered and over-hung with paper-
Backs in varying stages of disintegration*', damaged by an
Exchange-system – some thrillers, however, covert moral
Allegories, as with Graham Greene's '*entertainments*', not
Potboilers, a cut above proverbial green Penguins; then
Lascivious magazines inveigled by "*nerve-advertisements*" –
A cottage-industry catering for neurotics and sufferers
Of complexes – very deliberately punctuating triviality and
Thrills as if suggesting those who crave such must be
Privately inadequate; the '*thrill of naughtiness*' satiated by
These sensationalist weeklies, the accompanying illustrations
Replacing '*the photographic pin-ups*' are '*drawings*' done

'Originally in heavily-shaded pencilling... then photographed ... The artist, who usually works in the Varga idiom, can let Himself go... to produce a picture... boldly suggestive' with *'a Brassy vulgarity... rough... gusto, the Chaucerian touch'* – Mars Ravelo's Varga comic strip from the Filipino *Bulaklak Magazine* of the late Forties was owed a huge debt for its Ubiquitous, super-powerful influence over subsequent Publications – impossible to police such pornographic art; The *"blood-and-guts' sex-novelettes'* were everywhere like a Leaved virus, could be purchased *'not only from the 'magazine Shops' but from some railway-bookstalls... usually in a Corner... lying beneath the cards of aspirin and the styptic Pencils'* which showed how *'railway-reading can be a Release-valve'*; Hoggart glanced nostalgically to his Upbringing on comparatively tamer material which required Much more work from readers' imaginations: *'Novels by Writers with... French names'*, such explicit paperbacks well-Camouflaged: *'On the cover... the atmosphere is more Edwardian than mid-century... The cover-ladies... peep Through titles such as...* Dangerous Bliss... Passionate Nights *... soft and wilting victims on ottomans... in dressing-gowns'* Generating *'a nursemaid-naughtiness... sex of the boudoir... Wisps of lace and mouths in a moue'* – so much tamer than Mattress-temptresses of the present: *'In comparison with The cover-girls here, those of Pierre Laforgue are homely. These are the lush but 'gone wrong' descendants of those Varga girls who decorated servicemen's billets from Kirkwall To Kuala Lumpar. Their blouses sag permanently where The last attempt at rape was beaten off'*; the cheap prose is Notably a chip off the iceberg sensibility: *'... the style is Debased Hemingway... the images... catch the nerve-thrill... it Has the life of a cruel cartoon'*; anywhere is everywhere, Everything reduced to lowest common denominators not least In terms of morality, augmenting cut-price commonality in Vice and appetite... Such hedonism loosed from responsibility Led ultimately to solipsism, a *'diet of sensation without Commitment'* denying spiritual nutrition and all *'outside The limited range of... immediate appetites. Souls which...*

Have had little opportunity to open will be kept... turned in
Upon themselves, looking out... upon a world which is largely
A phantasmagoria of passing shows... vicarious stimulations
... a glassily hermaphrodite existence ('Life like a permanent
Wank ... inside you,')' as a young soldier put it graphically to
Hoggart, *'The predominant atmosphere during... National*
Service' – apart from the abundance of khaki autodidacts,
National Service, if anything, a melting-pot for anxious
Corporals since all male citizens no matter education, talents
Or interests had to do mandatory time in the services – cue
Scholastic milksop Lance Bombardier Evans in *Events*
While Guarding The Bofors Gun... The *'thrilling stories'*, prurient,
Blazing with *'Jezebels, as most advance trailers dub them'*;
Hoggart quoted Denis de Rougemont who argued villains
Triumphed emotionally even though in plot terms they
Always lost, carnality they excited, as mistresses, marked
Them out as alluring antagonists, betraying to tempted
Protagonists aridness of their marriages; unedifying fictions
Satisfying fantasies, primitive prose-appetites, eliciting *"stock*
Responses'... Not exploring... experience through language'...

XIV

On youth culture in the late Fifties, flick knife-wielding gangs
Aside: *'symptomatic'* are the *'juke-box boys... who spend*
Their evenings listening in harshly lighted milk-bars to
The 'nickelodeons" amid *'the nastiness of... modernistic*
Knickknacks' that mark *'aesthetic breakdown'* – not imitation
James Deans but milk-bar Russ Tamblyns in *'drape-suits'* and
With *'an American slouch'* listening to thin tinny music as
Broadcast on the Light Programme, *'Some of the tunes are*
Catchy; all have been doctored' with *'the 'hollow-cosmos'*
Effect which echo-chamber recording gives' – this must have
Been the very first youth subculture to have wallowed in
Bright lights rather than skulked in shadowy corners, marble-
White brightness of milk-bars to blares of jukeboxes (or, in

Board of Trade terminology, *'coin-operated phonographs'*):
*'... a peculiarly thin and pallid form of dissipation, a...
Spiritual dry-rot amid the odour of boiled milk'* – teen tots,
Brylcreemed babies in blaring nurseries; Hoggart singled
Them out as being markedly vulnerable to the *'debilitating
Mass-trends of the day'*, characterised them thus: *'no aim, no
Ambition... no belief... modern equivalents of Samuel Butler's
Mid-nineteenth-century ploughboys... vacant... ungainly...
Uncomely... apathetic'*; gifted more leisure time than any
Generation before yet at a loss as to how to fill it except in
Passive receptiveness to whatever trivialities available to
Them: *'The job is... done... by day... the rest is amusement...
There is time to spare and some money in the pocket... Society
... makes few demands on them – the use of their hands and of
A fraction of their brains for forty hours a week. For the rest
They are open to... entertainers and their... mass-equipment'*;
Hoggart described them in all their alienated ennui and
Estranged energies, the new young consumer classes, *'tamed
Helots of a machine-minding class'*, each one a *'hedonistic but
Passive barbarian'*; Hoggart *'compiled... a list of epithets'*
From newspaper editorials which signposted *'virtues and
Vices in the new canon. For the vices: pharisaical... dull;...
Mobbish;... mealy-mouthed; conventional; hypocritical...
Boring... For the virtues: new; different; unorthodox;...
Outspoken; wide-awake;... vigorous; zestful;... enterprising;...
Crusading; 'urchin grin'; candid; audacious; youthful;
Sincere'*; policing vocabularies, the Press claimed they were
Simply giving readers what they wanted, disingenuously
Neglecting to mention it is they who tell their readers what it
Is they want rather than spontaneous preferences – the sort
Of anti-culture in which a popular musician quoted by
Hoggart declared: *"I attribute my success to giving the people
What the people want"* swiftly followed by proleptic qualifier:
"I am not a snob"; Hoggart branded mass popular culture a
'Candy-floss world' whose producers were unconscionable
Transcribers of dumbed-down communication in the printed
Word where verbs were venerated, adjectives vetted; then
There were the *'popular writers'* and *'literary Department*

Stores', their '*rules-of-thumb... never to put in any 'boring Description*'... Hoggart took a pot shot at pot-boiler scribes
And hack writers of a kind who took Hemingway's '*iceberg*'
Sensibility to its unencumbered extreme: '*They can publish in Great quantity... without the phases which in a serious writer Mark developments in his... expression, because they write Semi-automatically... Not the attitude to language of The creative writer, trying to mould words into a shape which Will bear the peculiar quality of his experience*' but with '*a Facility with... stock phrases... they act as picture-makers*';
Hoggart's biggest beef was with those of his working-class
Contemporaries who were exponents of this pauperisation
Of prose, exploiters of their own exploitation: '*There is a Temptation among some social critics to see in... popular Literature... some... plot by 'the authorities'... of keeping The working-classes quietly doped. But many of those who Are doing... best... in this field are themselves of working-Class origin, products of the scholarship system*' (corporals
Of scholarship) '*If there is a plot, it is a remarkably cunning One*' – quite probably, behind their betrayal, an enabling
Establishment; '*These young men always insist... they 'really Belong to the people – share their laughter and tears*'' – how
Many would have known the word nostalgia originates from
The Greek *nostos* (*home*) and *algos* (*pain*), '*homesickness*',
Heimweh in German...? Hoggart knew there was much more
Baggage to the working-class '*scholarship boy*' made good, a
Psychological quagmire of anomie, which he detailed from
Personal experience in a section titled '*Unbent Springs: A Note on the Uprooted and Anxious*', which included an
Apposite excerpt from George Eliot's *Middlemarch*, on
Withered scholar Casaubon: '*... never to be liberated from A small hungry shivering self... always to be scholarly and Uninspired*'; as to the '*anxious and uprooted*' they are
Identified by their '*lack of poise*' and '*uncertainty*', are
'*Emotionally uprooted from their class*' which '*can lead them Into... self-consciousness*' and '*make it easy for a sympathiser To dramatise their angst)*', vulnerabilities exacerbated by
'*A physical uprooting from their class through... scholarship*';

They lead *'apparently normal lives but never without an Underlying... unease'*, summoning to mind Philip 'Pip' Pirrip From Dickens' *Great Expectations*; *'Almost every working-Class boy who goes through the process of... scholarships Finds himself chafing against his environment... He is at The friction-point of two cultures'* – also calling to mind Dennis Potter's Nigel Barton; Hoggart's empirical depictions Grew more intimate: *'He will have... to oppose the ethos of The hearth, the intense gregariousness of the working-class Family group'* where *'everything centres upon the living-room ... the bedrooms are cold... and to warm them or the front Room... would... be expensive'* and *'require an imaginative Leap... The boy has to cut himself off mentally... to do his Homework... Once at grammar-school, he quickly learns to Make use of a pair of different accents'*; but it can become A Casaubon-esque academic distance, a *'piling-up'* Of *'knowledge and received opinions'*, he *'becomes an expert Imbiber and doler-out'* who *'rarely discovers an author for Himself... He seems set to make an... unjoyous kind of clerk... Such a scholarship boy... does not acquire the unconscious Confidence of... a public-school-trained child... He has been Trained like a circus-horse, for scholarship winning... The driving-belt hangs loosely... from... the examination-Passing machine'* – lost without a *'certificate'* he cares too Much for *'marked and ticketed success'*; Hoggart brought in A passage from Graham Greene's *It's A Battlefield* (1934) Depicting hapless scholarship-sprung clerk Conrad Drover: *'Pale, shabby, tightly strung, he had advanced from post to Post in his insurance office with the bearing of a man about to Be discharged... Brains, like a fierce heat, had turned The world to a desert round him'*; a similar pathos in JB Priestley's depictions of office workers in *Angel Pavement* (1930) – on clerical relic Mr. Smeeth: *'... a grey drudge... Toiling... at figures of no importance... a creature of the little Foggy City street, of crusted ink-pots and dusty ledgers... a Typical troglodyte of... dingy... civilisation'*; and on insecure Clerk Harold Turgis: *'A thinnish, awkward young man, with a Rather long neck... You would not say he was ugly, but... it*

Would have been better... if he had been... Something about
His appearance... a lack of colour and bloom... suggested...
All the food he ate... rooms he sat in... clothes he wore, were
Wrong... His blue serge suit bulged... sagged and shone'...

XV

On self-improvers of whom Hoggart wrote partly empirically,
Partly empathically: '*... those who... ask questions of*
Themselves about their society, who are... 'Between two
Worlds, one dead, the other powerless to be born'. They are
The 'private facts in public places' among the working-classes
... Koestler's 'Thoughtful Corporals'... who take up... self-
Improvement.... They are to be found... among minor clerks...
Black-coated workers' but also among some blue collars –
Scholarly stonemason Jude was influenced in his formative
Awe for knowledge by Phillotson, his schoolmaster, who first
Pointed out to him the misty spires of Christminster, first
Of the two to taste bitter disappointment of thwarted ambition
Due to fixed social station; this rootless intellectual *'belongs*
Now to no class... not even to... the 'classless intelligentsia'';
He's the type likely to be called a *'potty professor'* by kith and
Kin, to display a *'gaucheness at practical things... His*
Compensatory claim to... be able to handle 'book-knowledge',
Is insecurely based', since books *'do not give him that power*
Of speech... which he seeks. He is as gauche there as with
The craftsman's tools'; he becomes an exile, a pariah, an
Outsider but has to keep moving forward and further away
From his background, longs for belonging, *'pines for some*
Nameless Eden where he never was' – for prelapsarian
Occupation; *'The nostalgia is... more ambiguous because he*
Is... in quest of his own absconded self yet scared to find it. He
... wants to go back... yet thinks he has gone beyond his class,
Feels himself weighted with knowledge... And this is only one
Of his temptations to self-dramatisation'; trying to ingratiate
Himself with his original peers doesn't work, he is a refugee

From his origins, an anomaly, quandary, misfit, mutation:
'If He tries to be 'pally' with working-class people, to show... he
Is one of them, they 'smell it a mile off'... immediately detect
The uncertainty in his attitudes'; he is always dogged by
Nostalgia in terms of its original meaning: homesickness;
'He has left his class, at least in spirit', is *'too tense and over-*
Wound. Sometimes the working-classes and... middle-classes
Can laugh together. He rarely laughs; he smiles constrainedly
With the corner of his mouth... with one part of himself he
Admires much he finds in' the middle-class: *'intelligence...*
Breadth of outlook... style'; like Jack London's Martin Eden,
Enchanted by the higher *'altitude of living'* of the cultivated
Even though it gives him a nervous vertigo, unable to grasp
Spinning opportunities to a point he can process them, kept
Outside by his efforts to escape past experience, his
Knowledge gives him no comfort, only estrangement; *'He*
Would like to be a citizen of that well-polished... book-lined...
Magazine-discussing world of the successful... middle-class
Which he glimpses through doorways or feels awkward
Among on short visits, aware of his grubby fingernails'; and
Like Martin Eden also finds appreciation of his new social
And cultural place spoilt by his peripheral perceptions made
Lopsided by a shoulder-chip: *'With another part of himself he*
Develops an asperity towards' this cultured world, *'turns up*
His nose at its self-satisfaction and earnest social concern...
Intelligent coffee-parties... suave sons at Oxford, and its...
Pretensions... He is Charles Tansley in Virginia Woolf's To
The Lighthouse', though might equally be Jude Fawley,
Martin Eden, Edwin Reardon, Frank Owen, Paul Morel, Harold
Turgis, Gordon Comstock, David Powlett-Jones, Nigel
Barton... There was no place to accommodate self-improvers,
No specially prepared social space to provide companionship
For them – and what companionship but simply other self-
Improvers sitting amid heaps of books in some reading-room
Purgatory green-lit by banker's lamps – if *'Hell is other*
People' as Jean-Paul Sartre put it in *Huis Clos*, then Purgatory
Must be other self-improvers; *'He has not the compensations*
Of a craftsman' nor *'of religious belief... He is earnest for self-*

Improvement, but not with the... eagerness... of the Mr
Lewishams who swotted at the Polytechnic and read Shaw
And Wells... His texts are... early Aldous Huxley... Kafka...

Toynbee. You are gifted from above with that which ordinary people have not got: you have your talent... talent places you apart... You have only one defect. Your false position... sorrow, and... catarrh of the bowels are all due to it. That is your... lack of education. ... *veritas magis amicitæ...* life has its conventions. In order to feel at ease among intelligent people... not to be a stranger among them... be overwhelmed by them, you must be to a certain degree educated...

One of a prolific crop of 'Pip' Pirrips with chips; *'He has*
Great aspirations, but not quite the equipment nor... staying-
Power to realise them. He would be happier... if he resigned
Himself... to being the moderately equipped person he is', but
In spite of himself feels he has some special purpose... Prior to
The Open University (pioneered under Harold Wilson's
Labour Government, 1969, cusp of the progressive Seventies),
Apart from Pelicans, the prime route to self-improvement was
Through correspondence courses advertised in various
Magazines and supplements, appealing to readers' educational
Insecurities, from *'general mental aids'* to the *'advertisements*
Offering the secret of fluent expression, of speaking like a
'... cultured individual'; the *'portmanteau guides to an over-all*
Culture' selling themselves with a sense of urgency like
Department store SALES: *'THIS CHANCE WILL NOT*
OCCUR AGAIN'... The tone of the announcements... suggests
The 'call to study' or to 'Culture' will be only allegorical... an
Almost magically quick method of removing an unformulated
... insufficiency'; Hoggart's grasp of reading habits of scholarly
Blue collars and clerkly intellectuals descriptively forensic as
A Sherlockian expository précis – so precise in its empiricism
As to seem almost mediumistic, clairvoyant eavesdropping:
'Others are proud of reading JB Priestley' and other *"serious*
Writers with a message'. Others have learned... Mr. Priestley

Is a 'middlebrow", so they read *'bitterly ironic or anguished Literature – Waugh, Huxley, Kafka, and Greene. They own The Penguin Selection from Eliot... subscribe to* Encounter. *They know a little... about Frazer and Marx;... probably own A copy of the Pelican edition of Freud's* Psychopathology Of Everyday Life. *They sometimes listen to... the Third Programme'...* On the interior life of rootless ones, uprooted Scholarship boys, blue collar bohemians, gentleman rankers, Anxious corporals pulled up by bootstraps, Hoggart came into His own: *'Some have a precarious tenancy in several near-Intellectual worlds'*, they *'read the* New Statesman and Nation *... know the arguments about the debasing effect of The popular press and... corruption of advertisements'* and *'Feel... they share something of the 'waste land'... the angst* [Of] *intellectuals; but will really be in a waste land of Their own'* – one almost always awash with ashtrays; some Achieve a polish, *"opinionation"*, warm to the glow Of *'borrowed ideas... on the H-Bomb... capital punishment... "The population problem"... a mental promiscuity'*, grasp *'A number of badly understood ideas, but on the whole feel Away. They read the reviews more easily than the books being Reviewed, and... take them as a... substitute'...* On the interiors In which self-improvers nurtured interior lives: *'They have... Lost the cluttered homeliness of their origins'*, *'are not... Chintzy'*, furnishings reflect their *'favourite styles in literature'* Making for *'self-conscious rooms'*, *'glossy ornaments and The patterned side of the curtains face the street'* like Windowed showrooms with *'an anonymous public air, similar To... utility furniture. So much is designed for... culturally Keeping up with the Koestlers'*; Hoggart noted snobbery Dished out towards these never-quite-upcoming self-Improvers by the literati and intelligentsia, as did EM Forster, eavesdropping on the preconceived judgement of one Of his characters in *Howard's End*: *'She knew the type so well – The aspirations, the mental dishonesty, the familiarity with The outside of books'*, harsh and more fitting for philistine Than culturally aspiring, as was Hoggart's judgement: *'... their urge for culture has... a grim and humourless air...*

Yet... at a time when it is so easy to be led into... low-browism,
Some retain... idealistic love for 'things of the mind'... as a
Substitute for... religious belief... Religion is suspect... culture
Is a sign of disinterested goodness' but they expect *'more from*
Culture than culture can give'; they are wrongtimers *'much*
Affected by their time' – some *'joined the Communist Party...*
Or the Left Book Club or... the Social Credit Party in
The thirties... 'Save his own soul he has no star' was applied
By Hardy to Jude the Obscure; but the light of the soul in
Today's Judes is... flickering and insecure', made so by all-
Pervasive persuasive voices, intrusive, convincing, confusing,
Contradictory, as *'sign-posts disappear into... mists of...*
Endless relativity: does anyone ever... act from principle?...
Are they simply in need of a tonic?'... Hoggart's anguished
Self-educators were *'emotionally inhibited'* by their fruitless '
Search for... belief... and its constant rebuttal', so some
Of them took up *'the game of finding clay feet'*; Hoggart
Diagnosed in this surface cynicism *'a nostalgia for belief'*;
Each scholarship boy undergoes *Bildungsroman* made
Tangible, *'a bruised consciousness'* for *'their roots have been*
Taken up for scrutiny too often; they have become... spiritual
Waifs and strays... they care... they stand for something' just
As society sits down on its settee, *'the population'* reduced to
'Receptive passivity... eyes glued to television sets'... In
The late Nineteenth century blue collar autodidacts, clerkly
Intellectuals, keen readers and anxious corporals had
Everything to look forward to, so much still to build:
'... people such as this... at great sacrifice supported Trade
Unionism... the Co-Operative Movement', they were *'pillars of*
Local chapels... helped... set up the Labour Representation
Committee... Their leaders... were men such as Tom Mann,
Ben Tillett, Keir Hardie and George Lansbury' (four Labour
Stalwarts all working-class autodidacts: sons of a clerk, ship's
Carpenter, miner, railway worker, respectively) – and what
Of their reading matter? *'Morris and Ruskin... Blatchford's*
Merrie England... *they subscribed to Blatchford's* Clarion *in*
The nineties... Some... joined Mutual Improvement Societies...
They bought the volumes in Morley's Universal Library and

Other cheap series... read Shaw and... Wells's Outline
Of History... *Watt's* Thinker's Library. *There were some... for*
Whom... Services' Education during the last war had real
Meaning'; self-improvers contemporary to Hoggart *'are in*
The habit... of buying copies of Pelicans... economic barriers
To knowledge have been largely removed, but there is still
A struggle to ignore the myriad... trivial and synthetic sirens';
Hoggart admired working-class autodidacts who after day
Shifts of hard physical graft spent evenings, even nights,
Exercising their minds *'in unpropitious conditions, inspired by*
A sense... of the power and virtue of knowledge', often esoteric
Knowledge outside their spheres of influence, ostensibly
Irrelevant to trades, thus discouraged by educational
Authorities: '... *a proposed class for dockers on Philosophy*
Had aroused interest locally but was refused by the relevant
Body... because 'the subject would not help Dockers"
(Expected to get their reading fixes from detective fiction);
Hoggart urged progressive-minded working-class minorities
Of his time to *'realise... the ideas for which their predecessors*
Worked are in danger of being lost, that material
Improvements can be used... to incline... working-people to
Accept a mean form of materialism as a social philosophy' –
That manifested eventually as Thatcherism – and *'the past will*
Be sold, culturally, behind their backs... It is harder to realise
Imaginatively the dangers of spiritual deterioration' and *'to*
Waken a great many from the hypnosis of immature emotional
Satisfactions... enjoyed by the very people... adversely affected
By them'; the hypnotised continued *'to put up with things'* with
A *'cheerfulness'* which was *'a self-conscious shadow of itself'*
But which still had the *'power to throw up comedians such as*
Norman Wisdom' and *'the exercise of cheerful debunking'*,
A regulated energy, arrested sense of urgency; but for most
Working-class men their repressed dreams, idealisms and
Deep need for harmony of hand and brain, for authentic
Occupation, was partially placated in *"handymanship'*:
'The counters of working-class paper-shops... crowded with...
The 'hobbies press'... cage-bird breeding, notably...
Budgerigars', while *'bird-fancying'* was most popular *'with*

Working-class people', the '*birds released from cane baskets*
By railway porters at the end of... platforms on Saturdays;
The owners, flat-capped' with stop-watches in hands, '*wait for*
Their pigeons to come softly out of the Saturday dusk' –
Feathered metaphors for deep repressed needs for escape from
Cramped parameters of lives and environments, vicarious
Aviation; for escape by land, the '*chara*' trip's '*spontaneous*
Urban adaptation'; and '*the public baths... smelly with*
Cleaning chemicals, chillingly angular... slippery-scummy at
The edges... ring shatteringly with... working-class children'...

XVI

To illustrate the hard-bitten spirit of an older working-class
Generation Hoggart described an old charlady he'd come to
Know in the late Forties so vividly as to form a mind-picture
Like an exquisite ink sketch out of *Mayhew's Characters*:
'*The rougher... 'Knees Up, Mother Brown' type... Her clothes*
... picked up... from second-hand-clothing shops... Over a...
Grubby blouse and skirt' she wore '*an ex-army gas-cape... She*
Must have been in her middle Forties... her face... scored with
Hard work [and] lines which... doggedness [and] overriding
Bravado bring. Her left eye had a violent cast and her lower
Lip a drop to the right so that on the whole the bravado won.
But it was a farouche *bravado... Her hair was a dirty mouse*
Colour, hanging... straggly... from... an old felt hat... rammed
... unshapenly to the head"; Hoggart's observations thorough
As Sherlockian deductions: '*Her shoes were split...; her lisle*
Stockings hung in circles from the knees. Her voice was
Raucous... by backyard 'callings'... and 'bawlings-out'... She
Was without subservience or deference... She asked those she
Worked for 'Not to mention it to the Guardians", possessed
Some typical '*working-class qualities*': '*... larger than life, as*
In a cartoon – their ability not to permit themselves to be
Altered'... How Hoggart captured the shabby-baroque
Appearance of the charlady – who might be seen as bohemian

In more cultured circles – was reflected in the kind of baroque
Working-class tastes he described under the heading
*'The Biggest Aspidistra in the World'. Excursions Into
The 'Baroque"*; in terms of architectured exteriors, an
Aesthetic attitude of mind which *'requires' 'sprawling, highly-
Ornamental, rococo extravagance. The 'baroque'... It loves
The East... perfumes should come from the Orient'*, cinemas
Aped theatres with exotic-sounding names suggesting *'a
Splendour... European... The commissionaires... look like
Ruritanian generals... moulded false-fronts of the* Plaza...
The Alhambra... *the* Embassy... *vie with one another'* – as for
Proletarian interiors: *'Basic furnishings are surmounted by
Articles'* of *'high colour... The older forms... look almost
Grotesque... The wallpaper... still has a bold pattern...
Decorated sea-shells are disappearing from... mantelpieces'*,
The *'vivid clip-rug'* selectively in evidence, everywhere
The *'highly-polished... stuff the neon-strip stores sell. Gone...
The lush Aspidistra in its... lush bowl... fed on aspirins and
Weak tea when it flagged'*, but its *'window-space'* usurpers
Spoke *'the same emotional language'*, and for the tea spread,
Articles of ritual: *'Plastic gewgaws... teapots shaped like
Country cottages... complicated lace-paper d'oyleys... lace
Half-curtains, crocheted table-runners... 'fancies' (curiously
Constructed and coloured little cakes)'*, pink and yellow-
Chequered Battenbergs sealed in yellow marzipan; in
The working-class styled ornaments and crafts, *'grotesqueries
Of fretwork... the Houses of Parliament in matchsticks...
The duchess sets and tea-cosies and poker-work'* (like Auden,
Hoggart imbued objects with symbolism by sanctifying them
With the definite article); the shabby-baroque could easily tip
Into the tacky, gaudy and garish, a throwback contrast to
Outdated Victorian and Edwardian tendencies still clung to by
The working class, pace cultural lag, contrasting literally like
Two different time periods to the smooth curvaceous Art
Deco and Modernist public precincts steeped in new
Stylishness frequented by middle classes, the *'cleaner lines of
The twentieth century'*, perfectly sculpted telephone kiosks,
Curved-butter bus stations; *'But in the working-class shopping*

... areas the old idiom... persists... in the huge furniture stores
... marzipan super-cinemas', each class had its part of the city
Centre which *'geographically... overlap'* but have *'distinctive*
Atmospheres... shops... tram stops, parts of the market, places
Of amusement, places for cups of tea', and tea was paramount,
A panacea in a cup (slurped by some from saucers), classless
Nectar, worshipful leaf, ubiquitous ambrosial brew variably
Browned with milk... Hoggart saw working-class districts as
Stuck in an Edwardian time warp, *'drably baroque'*, shop
Windows a *'tangle of odds-and-bobs at coppers each'* and
'The outer walls... a mass of small advertisements... in all
Stages of wear-and-tear, some piled a quarter of an inch
Thick'; because of financial lack the working class preferred
'Flowery chintz and bits of shiny brass'... The once-in-a-blue-
Moon big day out, almost sacred excursion of extravagance
Undertaken in brightly coloured charabancs, *'de-luxe*
Coaches', almost always to seaside resorts though the focus
Of the trip was the carriage: *'... the day-trip by 'chara'...*
Particularly taken up by working-class people... one of
Their peculiar... kinds of pleasure-occasion... in its garishness
... the 'chara' trip... speaks the language of: Oh, I do like to be
Beside the seaside' – invariably Bognor or Margate; *'These*
Buses... are the super-cinemas of the highways... plushily...
Upholstered'; stop offs at *'fish-and-chip saloons'* tiled like
Public toilets, generally *'making a splash'*; trips often
Culminated with end-of-pier pantomimes spiced with saucy
Postcard tropes and call-and-response participation; then
Bingo – and bottles of stout on the ride home to pie-eyed
Choruses of *'O didn't we have a luverly time...'*, a *'knees up'*,
A piece of *'secular music'* recalling music halls contrapuntal
To choiring chapels and the *'still lively oratorio tradition...*
'Bird In a Gilded Cage'... Some of the qualities displayed in
'Workers' Playtime', and 'Works' Wonders', but not in... tepid
Glucose-and-water of... other radio musical programmes for
Workers, which are not of the people, but... done for
The people'; Hoggart produced sublime musicological
Insights: *'... the beat of an old-fashioned waltz... is the beat of*
'A good weep'... a warm and pally feeling... a heavy nostalgia

... *sentimental ballads... 'If You Were The Only Girl In The World'... 'Little Dolly Daydream'... 'Lily Of Laguna', 'Roses of Picardy"* and, by contrast in mood, the up-tempo number, *'It Wasn't the girl I saw you with at Brighton"*, the *'rough... Battered old types: 'Two Lovely Black Eyes', 'I'm One of The Ruins that Cromwell Knocked About A Bit"*, and *'communal Roar'* of *'Ta-Ra-Ra-Boom-De-Ay'*... gutsy intergenerational Sing-alongs – *'Oh, For The Wings of a Dove', 'The Rugged Old Cross', 'glutinous... styles of singing'*; occasional Gloominess could be self-mocking: *'Mona Lott in 'Itma"* had A *'catch-line... 'It's bein' so cheerful as keeps me goin", Delivered in a graveyard voice'* – Hoggart coined a darkly Comic aphorism: *'... dissatisfaction* [is] *out-of-date... as Though one should wander through a holiday-camp... with Kafka in the pocket... and occasional hollow laugh'* – music With *'vigour... 'syncopated out... in favour of a drumming Mass-call... escape from personality and choice'* – Reconstituted stoicism meets the melodramatic: *'Diamond Bracelets Woolworth doesn't sell, baby', 'love... will outlast... The stars themselves'... quasi-religious language for... praise Of human love'*: religious songs as *'disguised love-songs'*; Song-books recalled old scrolling garlands of *"Long-songs"*...

XVII

Other than brain-investment in books a trade was the surest Way out from poverty, to *"have a trade in your hands'... The skilled workman... is out of the ruck of those who receive The first shock of... labour cuts; he has remnants of A journeyman's pride'* – one thinks of conscientious Frank Owen, Marxist signwriter in Robert Tressell's *The Ragged Trousered Philanthropists* who, after being forced by Circumstance to work as a painter-and-decorator for a firm Of cowboy builders, is given a one-off commission to paint A sign, something he feverishly savours in spite of it paying Little extra, because it satisfies his heart, mind and hands; one

Of the most debilitating and inhibiting of attitudes best not to
Retain from a working-class background which would only
Enfeeble self-improvement was the fatalistic *'dull dog-in-the-
Manger refusal to accept anything higher than one's own
Level of response'*; such fatalism difficult to shake off,
Timeworn adages had taken hold of tongues for too long:
"Oh, it'll all be the same in a hundred years' time'; this
Working-class complacency was scored with stoicism:
*'Not so Much the cheerfulness of the stiff upper lip as of
The unsuspecting, partly stoic, partly take-life-as-it-comes
'Lower orders'. TS Eliot says... stoicism can be... a refusal to
Be humble before God: working-class stoicism is rather a
Self-defence, against being... humbled before men'...* Though
Grounded in physical realities the working classes put much
Stock by intuition and superstition, whether reading tea leaves
(As if some hereditary residue of gypsies), window-shopping
Horoscopes or pinning all hopes on *'pools coupons'*, poor
Coupon hopefuls – *'One advertisement by a pools firm...
Shows a young man spurned by the girls... filling in his...
Coupon... and dispatching it... It is an advertisement of an
Acquisitive society'*; and a semi-articulated superstitious tilt to
Fate and destiny *'in... reports of what the stars foretell... in...
The electric fortune-telling machines at the seaside, in the tea-
Leaves and palm-of-hand readers of which every district
Throws up a few... in* Old Moore's Almanack' replete with
'Cabbalistic cover' and *'football pools forecasts'* where
'The recurrent word... is "luck"' and there's *'hope for
The sudden chance of fortune from heaven... the plethora of
Gambles and flutters... lucky draws... raffles... club lotteries'*;
But proletarians were also rationalists, pragmatists,
Philosophers-on-the-hop with plenty of aphorisms: *"Life is no
Bed of roses'... 'Tomorrow will take care of itself"*, Hoggart
Saw the working classes as *'cheerful existentialists'* – though
They were rather, happy fatalists: *'... the unplanned nature of
Life, the moment-to-moment meeting of troubles or taking of
Pleasure; schemes are mostly short-term'*, mottoes empirical,
Adages galore, wisdom empirically grimed but always a
Sunny side, a sense of fun, *'a kind of hedonism'* which deems

Life bearable *'so long as the big worries (debt, drink,*
Sickness) keep away', as in 'Billy's Weekly Liar *their banner-*
Motto might be "Smile Dammit Smile!"'... Self-improvement
Wasn't about one-upmanship, most had no truck with
Competitiveness for sake of feeling superior – fundamental to
Everything a sense of commonality bordering on inflexibility,
Conformity, advertisers' *'appeal to the ordinary'*: ' ... *if you*
Infringe the taboos you will run into disfavour: there's such a
Thing as mass thought... If you think the same as the man next
To you, you're all right. But... if you're seen bringing in a
Book [i.e. into work] or anything like that you're not' – like
The typical anxious corporal, always a class-pariah; Hoggart
Caught himself: '... *one runs the risk of resurrecting...*
The ghost of the noble savage, the simple unspoiled son of
Toil, fully equipped with finely discriminating organs (so
Much less... corrupt than... tired sophisticates who think)'
When noting *'working-class people can make quick*
Impressionistic judgements of great skill', adding this could in
Certain circumstances volt into naivety, that *'if... deceptively*
Approached under the correct flags' they *'can be as babies'* –
Gullible to reboiled *'blue collar'*-baiting electioneering fibs,
Vulnerable to wolves and Conservatives... Was it possible to
Appreciate poetic qualities in life when perceptions were so
Rooted in the concrete? Working-class speech was rich in
Physical descriptions but almost entirely unmetaphorical;
'Most working-people are non-political and non-metaphysical
In... outlook', their opinions generally *'unexamined... orally-*
Transmitted tags, enshrining generalisations... elevated by
Epigrammatic phrasing into... maxims' which have *'hypnotic*
And final effect, the sound of revealed truth, of... cracker-
Mottoes: "They're all talk –They've never done a day's work in
Their lives"; existence a constant bombardment of demands
Made in distancing middle-class English: *'They are assailed*
By a mass of abstractions... asked to... study 'good citizenship'
... have in mind the 'common good'. In most cases the appeals
Mean nothing... The local and concrete world is what can be
Understood... trusted' – Hoggart found an Auden quote to
Impress his point: *'Adjusted to the local needs of valleys/*

Where everything can be touched or reached by walking';
Their homes concrete refuges from this hostile metaphorical
World *'carved out under the shadow of... giant abstractions'*,
Not for them the *'literary life', or 'the life of the spirit"*, but
'Sport and Royalty' sufficed *'because... easily translated into...
Concrete terms,'* and courtesy of gossipy red tops, a false
Familiarity as Royals referred to by first names, *'Some girls
Find a glamour in the Royal family similar to... film-stars'*,
While to ambivalent husbands it smacked of *'special parades
In the services, of 'Blanco and bullshit"*; daily reading matter
Feeds these self-defeating fetishisms: *'The news-presentation
Of... Sunday gossip papers... belongs to the realms of
Imaginative or fictional writing of a low order'*; magazines
And comics spiced the working-class reading experience with
Snippets of infantilised information – but for all their gaudy
Colours and eye-catching logos, their poor quality paper
Betrayed the musty scent of intellectual decay and neglect,
'... roughly textured newsprint' that smells *'damp and fungoid'*,
Just *'a few kinds of type are used'*, covers *"flat' and boldly
Coloured in a limited range'*, punchy titles – *'Lucky Star,
The Miracle, The Oracle'*; brainwashing advertisements
Punctuating texts with lifestyle tips, commodity-fetishism:
*'Cosmetics... use an aristocratic appeal... The same ailments
Appear so often... a hasty generaliser might conclude...
The working-classes are congenitally... constipated and
'Nervy"... announcements of cures for disabilities'* – glossy
Paged thaumaturgy; the *'Scientists tell us'* trope shares space
With its superstitious 'Gypsy' progenitor... The working
Classes navigated margins with empirical compasses, if class-
Conscious then in comprehending the *'Us'/'Them'* paradigm,
Not something extrapolated but very real, concrete in
Their lives, never more so than when negotiating agents
Of pecuniary policing: *'The Means Test Official, the man from
'The Guardians', and the Employment Exchange Officer'* –
Looming figures in an anguished mythology of struggle:
*'A shadowy... powerful group affecting their lives at... every
Point:... the people who give you your dole, call you up...
Made you split the family in the thirties to avoid a reduction*

In the Means Test Allowance'; ordinary folk stalked by giants
Of indignity and indigence; small wonder '*working-class*
People... seem not 'oncoming' to social workers' and '*give*
Answers... to put off'; stigma of being '*on the parish*',
Ingrained ignominy of '*going on the Lloyd George*'; Hoggart's
Empirical Microscopic Observation picked up on aspects only
Those from the working class could recognise: '*Many old*
Working-class women have an habitual gesture' which '*DH*
Lawrence remarked... in his mother', and Hoggart recalled in
His grandmother: '*... a repeated tapping of her fingers on*
The arm of her chair... which accompanied an endless
Working out of something in her head' – domestic rumination;
Or '*a rhythmic smoothing of the hand down the chair-arm, as*
Though to smooth everything out and make it workable' or '*a*
Working of the lips or a steady rocking. None of these could
Be called neurotic gestures... they help the constant
Calculation'; Hoggart remembered his grandmother not
Grasping the figurative yet spouting aphorisms like Anglo-
Saxon poetry: "*There are some who become bitten-in and*
Make it all a harsh ritual and their toil a badge of dreadful
Honour"; few could match working-class anecdotes for force
And colour, and theatre: '*... the simplest... told dramatically*
With... rhetorical questions', emphatic pauses, '*alternations of*
Pitch'; so much tattered poetry in housekeeping, no chores or
Ragged rituals too spirit-stripping or soul-destroying for
Poetry: '*There are often difficulties of drying-space*' and '*a*
Complicated system of putting the damp stuff round the fire
On a clothes-horse and taking it off again into a basket or
Zinc bath'; like LS Lowry, Hoggart could see the grubby
Beauty in urban decay: '*... uniform houses intersected by...*
Ginnels and snickets (alley-ways) and courts [in] permanent
Half-fog; a study in shades of dirty-grey... Terraces are gap-
Toothed with sour... brick-bespattered bits of wasteground'
And at some distance '*a clinkered six-acre stretch surrounded*
By works and grimy pubs... a large red-brick urinal at its
Edge'... if not the fifth circle of Hell, a proletarian Purgatory
Where crammed home-dwellings, strung together with rags
Of laundry, '*are fitted into... dark... canyons between... giant*

Factories... goods-lines pass on embankments' by *'bedroom*
Windows... viaducts interweave with... railway lines and...
Canals', and *'pubs and... Methodist Chapels stick up at*
Intervals' – hubs for imbibing beer or spiritual gins; *'Rough*
Sooty grass rushes through... trampled earth-heaps' littered
With *"dog-muck', cigarette packets... ; rank elder, dirty*
Privet, and rosebay willow-herb take hold in... walled-off
Space behind the Corporation Baths'; stale air thick with
Industrial sounds and odours: *'Factory hooters, trains*
Shunting, the stink of the gas-works' marking time with
'Clockings-in-and-out'; Hoggart's painterly descriptions
Painstakingly detailed, dripping with sense-impressions:
'Misty evenings of March... beer-and-Woodbine smell of...
Men... cheap-powder-and-cream smell of... grown-up sisters...
Fresh starchiness of new clothes at Whitsun... aura of urine –
Dog, cat, and human' – and aural: *'Families talking...*
Laughing or quarrelling'; Dutch auctions on the stump
Policed by fag-butt-puffing bailiffs, each ash-tapped, evicted
Face brushed past, *'a horsehair sofa displaced by a modern*
One on hire purchase'... Hoggart, social lepidopterist, pinned
Down every variety of self-improver, many of whom were
Autodidacts by default, or serendipity, depending on opinion –
Whether by dint of being widowers, pensioners, or
Unemployed, temporarily or permanently, or simply misfits: *'...*
They come in off the streets... twisting scarves round
Collarless necks... solitaries, men whose... wives have died or
Are bedridden... scrabble along on a pension in a common
Lodging-house or in one room of an apartment-house in a
Démodé district... The older ones haunt... railway-stations' –
Through images and metaphors Hoggart the poet waxed
Lyrical on urban decay and down-at-heel shabby-genteel of its
Reverent refuges such as foot-shuffling, paper-ruffling,
Whispery book-churches of public libraries: *'It all... recalls*
Those hidden inlets... the smaller detritus of a river eventually
Reaches, held there in a yeasty scum – old sticks, bits of...
Paper, a few withered leaves, a matchbox. But the reading-
Rooms... have a syringed and workhouse air:... newspapers
Stretch bleakly around the walls, heavily clamped... sporting-

Pages... pasted over... magazines lie on dark-oak desks across
Which green-shaded lamps throw so narrow a beam...
The whole of the room above elbow height is in permanent
Shadow by... late afternoon' – a Rembrandtian atmosphere;
'The shadow helps to soften... notices, heavy black on white',
And, as in all churches, there are the moral Commandments,
As Hoggart noted in one he frequented: *'... eight major*
Injunctions, varying in length from SILENCE in letters nine
Inches high [to] READERS MUST CONFINE THEMSELVES
TO THE PUBLICATIONS... DISPLAYED. They range in tone
From the curtly peremptory to the interdictory'; Hoggart
Turned Hogarthian: *'... refuge of the misfits and left-overs...*
The hollow cheeked, watery-eyed, shabby, and... sad...
A pinched unmarried brother, kept by a married sister for...
His war-pension... an aged widower... smelling permanently
Of... frying-pan'; some *'plot how to win on the pools or*
Mumble through a rough sandwich; some turn leaves
Aimlessly or stare blankly... seeing each other daily but with
No contact... no conscious arts for social intercourse', most
'Dream of... warm fires... regular meals... cigarettes'; citing
EM Sargaison's *Growing Old In Common Lodgings*: *'Of*
The old men in a Belfast reading-room... 'Some... take
The opportunity of surreptitiously drying their socks on
The hot pipes, but banishment to the cold outside is... penalty';
Cigarettes accounted for much working-class outgoings –
Gaspers were essential punctuators of proletarian experience,
Sparking up was a coming up for air from cramped psychical
Parameters of existence, most anxious corporals plumed like
Troopers while ploughing through passing clouds of books...

XVIII

What was it choked off the growth of knowledge-hungry
'Thoughtful corporals' among the working classes...? What
Was it ensured over time simultaneous to the material
Mutation of the proletariat towards greater affluence would

Come the philistinification of mass culture, and the Tory
Trustification of the working classes...? In 1968 Robert
McKenzie and Allan Silver published a monograph which
Attempted to answer such questions, *Angels in Marble:
Working Class Conservatives in Urban England*, which began
By focusing historically on the Tories' politically
Opportunistic Second Reform Bill 1867 under Derby and
Disraeli to extend the franchise to urban labouring man –
A policy so culturally sensitive it was even impeached in
A poem by Coventry Patmore – to which Tory historian
Homersham Cox opined at the time the irony that *'The policy
Of political 'leaps' remained to be invented by a government
Which calls itself Conservative'* far from the party's normal
Caterpillar drag from *'precedent to precedent'* in *'slow and
Heedful steps'*; with unbound snobbery Cox recoiled at
The prospect of working-class voters, noting *'hopeful Tories
Think the very poor class will be amenable to the influence of
Their superiors, and so the country will be saved from
Democracy'* – an undisguised admission Britain was far from
A representative parliamentary democracy, but simply
A glorified fiefdom of entrenched hegemonies, *'rotten
Boroughs'*, plutocracy; Cox mocked promise of the upcoming
Dispensation as potentially permitting *'not merely household
... – but hovel suffrage'*, many other Tories agreeing, who had
Heeded Karl Marx's optimistic prediction that because
The English proletariat far outnumbered the ruling class its
Partial enfranchisement was golden opportunity for turning
The class system upside down, would inevitably lead to
The ultimate political supremacy of the proletariat but
Tragically reckoned without taking into account the Satanic
Cunning of Conservatism, duplicitous Tory rhetoric, and
Equally chronic proletarian sense of self-defeating deference
And respect for their *'betters'* – deference, the English
Disease, would prove eventually resistant to the only briefly
Effective socialist vaccine – England, at least, an effortlessly
'*Deferential* nation'... But even Liberals of the time were
Resistant to complete enfranchisement of the labouring
Classes, such as Walter Bagehot, openly contemptuous

Of the Tories' resistance to electoral reform for simply being
About the *'fear of the loss of property'*; but Bagehot was
Afraid of the burgeoning vanguard of voters, of *'rule of mere
Numbers'*, and, as with the Tories, had no wish to see
A newfangled American-style *'democracy'* washing up on
English shores – or worse still, a republic; *'The generality of
Englishmen'*, he remarked in *The English Constitution*, were
Not fit for *'elective government'*, he most of all advocated an
Avoidance of *'the supremacy of ignorance over instruction
And of numbers over knowledge'* – along the lines of Richard
Hoggart's later concerns about lowest-common-denominator
Cultural democracy at the fag-end of the Fifties; Bagehot had
Supported the 1832 extension of the franchise (which also
Banned *'rotten boroughs'*) but warned any further extension
Would result in *'a House of Commons made up of opposites'*
(Which one might think to be the point!) *'a more militant
Radicalism confronting a less intelligent Conservatism'*;
Bagehot snobbishly warned that *'newly enfranchised workers
Would not 'defer the same way to wealth and rank, and to
The higher qualities of which these are the rough symbols...
If you once permit the ignorant classes to rule you may bid
Farewell to deference for ever'* (how wrong to underestimate
The masochistic tenacity of English deference); Disraeli, more
Enlightened of Tory minds, threw off such hysterical
Resistances, accusations of a *'great betrayal'*, trembling
Jeremiads, assuring naysayers there was nothing *'to fear by
Bringing the working class within the pale of the constitution'*
... But in spite of opening up the franchise the moneyed and
Propertied still monopolised power, since *'membership in
Parliament carried... no stipend... a serious handicap'* for
Poorer candidates – in 1900 *'a number of trade unions joined
With three tiny socialist sects to form the Labour
Representation Committee. By 1906, a... self-styled Labour
Party won 29 seats in the House of Commons, and after
The Second World War... supplanted the Liberals as... second
Party... Thus the enfranchisement of the working classes,
Which Lord Cranbourne saw... as a fatal (and self-inflicted)
Blow to the Conservative Party, in fact helped... ensure*

The downfall of the Liberals'; it further demonstrated how
The Tories (their name derived from *tóraí*: Irish for *outlaw*)
Seemed to have the luck of the Devil; '*The Labour Party
Proved to be a far less formidable opponent than
The pessimistic Tories... had assumed, since in
The intervening forty-four years... it managed on only one
Occasion (1945) to win a clear working majority*', while,
Since 1885, the Tories' electoral success was unrivalled by
Any other political party in Europe; almost in spite
Of themselves they had proven inadvertently progressive
Having '*through a strange sequence of events played a major
Role in... transferring potential control of the machinery of
Government to the urban industrial masses*'; far from being
What John Stuart Mill disparaged as '*the stupid party*',
The Tories' stratagem had paid off and would keep paying
Dividends, events ever seemed to benefit them, as history
Often benefits those on the wrong side of it; Labour had
Replaced the Liberals as Opposition, but would themselves be
Broken '*by the events of 1931... In 1951... the Conservatives
Resumed power and began the longest... span of office*
[Of] *any British Party... in a century*'; it seemed the only
Periodically interrupted Tory monopoly on power was a
Symptom of its supreme patriotism in spite of occasional
Chameleonism, and its relative stability, since, inescapably,
'*Parties of the left, the parties of movement and change, are
More likely to develop fissiparous tendencies than... those
Whose principal aim is to conserve the status quo*'; the British
Left seemed destined to protracted disappointment having
Underestimated proletarian deference, '*From the first
Enfranchisement of the working classes in 1867 the left has
Awaited the day... 'the people would awaken''...*

Engels. What do you say to the elections in the factory districts? Once again the proletariat has discredited itself terribly... It cannot be denied that the increase of working class voters has brought the Tories more than their simple percentage increase... (*1868*)

After Labour's loss of office following the surprise result
Of 1951, Peter Shore wrote in a Labour Party pamphlet:

Shore. The question which must now be asked is why the fruits of universal suffrage have taken so long to ripen. How is it that so large a proportion of the electorate, many of whom are neither wealthy nor privileged, have been recruited for a cause which is not their own?

Such quandary would ring through the decades and well into
The next century... *'Labour's second clear working majority*
(Won in 1966) was heralded... as the beginning of the long
Delayed era' – yet time and again Conservatism was
Resuscitated back to twitching life – or its imitation –
A Frankenstein's monster, to stifle futures, pettifog Progress,
A *'minority creed'* with a knack at capturing majorities...
Part of the Tories' pulling power, its monopoly on patriotism,
Which led Quintin Hogg MP to declare in 1967 *'Being*
Conservative... is only another way of being British', while Tory
Leader and Prime Minister 1902–05, Arthur Balfour,
Proposed *'The great unionist party should control, whether in*
Power or in Opposition, the destinies of this great Empire';
Its will to power, capacity to adapt, ensured its longevity, less
Episodic, more permanent grasp on power, so, having
Espoused *'the collective power of society to redress... social*
Wrongs caused by economic development' laying *'emphasis*
On man as a producer with duties to his fellow men' in
Response to the nineteenth century *'Liberal doctrine of*
Laissez-faire' which *'exalted man as a consumer and his*
Individual rights'; the Tories toed the line of the more
Economically cooperative post-war consensus after wresting
Power back from Attlee's Labour, Churchill capitulating to
Keeping certain industries nationalised even though it *'may...*
Mar the symmetry of party recrimination' – though there were
Detractors of such adaptability who'd argue the party was
Unscrupulous in its pursuit of power, having overly supple
Principles, so it was given the epithet of *'an organised*

Hypocrisy'; philosophically, the Tory party was Manichean in
Its deeply pessimistic view of the imperfectability
Of humankind in an earthly material realm, so many came to
'*The ultimate Conservative view*' as Oakeshott put it:
'*The world is the best of all possible worlds, and everything in
It is a necessary evil*'; Kenneth Pickthorn wrote in 1952:
'*Conservatives have constantly warned... what each
Generation has to conserve is immensely more valuable...
Than what any one generation can hope to create*', hence
The need '*to conserve*' at the core of their name and purpose,
And yet '*Conservatives never tire of the analogy which
Compares society to a tree... have accepted... growth and
Change*'; rather than a dogma or doctrine, Toryism was an
'*Attitude*', '*temperament*', '*mood*', '*habit of mind*', took
The most pessimistic aspects to Christian doctrine,
Particularly antinomianism (predestination of Saved and
Damned) by which it appeared, like Puritanism, to sanctify
Accrual of capital (Mammon), excusing the cupidity, gluttony
And indulgences of privileged elites – touches of the fire-and-
Brimstone Baptist pulpit: '*Man is sinful... imperfectible, prone
To wickedness and... evil doing*', that human society is
The '*inherited social framework which constrains his...
Brutishness and... Anarchy. For one generation of men to set
About remaking the social framework to some blueprint
Devised by* a priori *reasoning is an unthinkable invitation to
Disaster*'; Edmund Burke's take on Toryism was almost a
Form of curatorship: he believed society was "*a partnership...
Between those who are living... those who... are dead, and
Those who are to be born*'... *their surest guide to how they
Should attend to the affairs of the society of which they are,
Momentarily, living members*' – but this was a very different
Dictum to Marx's '*tradition of all the dead generations...
Weighs like a nightmare on the brain of the living*': for
The Tory "*the tradition of all the dead generations*' *is
The revelation, through history, of God's purpose among men*'
And in the spirit of *felix culpa* to ensure the experiment
Of existence is a perpetual happy fault, adaptive but
Fundamentally unchanging; '*Society... has evolved over time,*

A harmonious and organic union, 'a fixed compact... [of] all ... moral natures each in their appointed place' – Toryism
Aimed at *'social unity'* but this meant keeping the social
Hierarchy intact, with manageable smattering of mobility; as
Accepting the so-called *'post-war consensus'*, the Tories could
*'Refute... charges either of opportunism or of hypocrisy with
Respect to their support of the modern welfare state'* by
Claiming that their (pliable) *'principles'* were *'entirely
Compatible with... full state responsibility for social welfare'* –
Though Thatcherism stamped out such briefly flourishing
Social democratic *esprit de corps* from the party;
Conservative leader and repeat Prime Minister Stanley
Baldwin wrote that the British Constitution *'could never have
Been created: it is the result of centuries of evolution and
Native in its growth... This tradition is... our greatest
Safeguard'*; but many Tories *'suffered repeated failures of
Nerve in the course of... 'democratisation' of the constitution'* –
Their main fear was Socialism, the growing threat
Of egalitarianism only kept at bay by gestures of euergetism;
Tories had *'never made any secret of their belief in the innate
Inequality of men... they have nothing but contempt for social
Doctrines which preach... equality. This they dismiss as
'Intellectual and biological nonsense''*; on inequality they've
Always been sanguine: *'... inequality of natural ability
Necessarily results in class'* – supremely disingenuous: most
Class was and still is anchored in ancestral inheritances,
Anything but meritocracy of talents; Tories believed *'a system
Of social classes is not merely inevitable'* but *'also desirable...
An... adjunct of human nature... If a* [classless] *society were
Possible it would be as useless as a rankless army'* or *'a wine-
List that gave neither the name of the vineyards nor the date
Of the vintages'*... Toryism has ever thrown the chicken bone
Of *'social mobility'* as half-baked incentive to more materially
Ambitious proletariat to cooperate in their own oppression on
Promise some of them might have opportunity to escape it; it
Claimed some *'indispensable criteria – character, ability,
Moral standard – are inheritable... the tested chain of
Essential aristocracy'*; Bagehot articulated fundamentals

Of Toryism in a fit of self-lacerating honesty: *'Nothing more Nor less than fear... it finds expression... in excellent Sentences as to the safety of society,' (the protection of the) 'Results of ages... – that those who feel it dread that Their shop, their house, their life – not so much their physical Life as their whole mode and sources of existence – will be Destroyed and cast away... Anyone with anything to lose, if it Is only the opportunity to be idle – these are... Conservatives'*;
Most important to the Tories, apart from maintaining status
Quo and monarchy, were rights of property, not far removed
From American Paul Elmer More's edict: *'To the civilised Man the rights of property are more important than the right To life'* – Keith Feiling framed the matter more critically in
What Is Conservatism? (1930): *'... guardian of order... kind Nurse of our affections... nourisher of our personality... it was The sin of our fathers, who did not harness this... vital Principle to universal enjoyment but 'let things find Their level,' covering with their blameless white flower this Whited sepulchre of fact abused. Whence came the scandal of The slums... all the time... Victorian drawing rooms piped up, 'I'll sing thee Songs of Araby,' they were manufacturing The street Arab'*; but ultimately *'Conservatives do insist... Abuses associated with the institution of property in no way... Counterbalance its... beneficent attributes. Property was seen By Burke to be vested with an almost spiritual quality'*, while
To Baldwin it was *'something in the eternal world which is a Material representation of human personality"* – which
Almost smacked of Neoplatonism; antiquated notions as to
'Landholder' as *'sheet anchor of... community'*; while Tory
Hatchet critic John Wilson Croker *'claimed... 'the territorial Interest' was in the political world the equivalent of gravity in The physical, keeping things in place and preserving order'*...
Tories continued through the nineteenth century to espouse
Propertied principles and doubted *'factory-owning and shop-Keeping stimulated... equivalent virtues'* – they *'took up Bagehot's position on property: 'if it has been inherited, it Guarantees education; if acquired, it guarantees ability"* –
Ability at land-grabbing; McKenzie and Silver excavated

Their own figurative and allusive take: '*... property has... Qualities of Ithuriel's spear, which healed the very wounds it Inflicted; the... rapid accumulation of property may damn its Possessor, but... passed on by inheritance, will save his Descendants*', so Tories accepted plutocrats '*in the confidence ... they would... sire gentlemen*'; Tories were suspicious Of politics and in part set up their party to police it – as Quintin Hogg MP put it: '*Conservatives do not believe... Political struggle is the most important thing in life. In this They differ from Communists, Socialists, Nazis, Fascists, Social Creditors, and... the British Labour Party. The simplest Among them prefer foxhunting – the wisest religion*', and see Men as under a "*cosmological' rather than... political order*'; RJ White wrote that Toryism's mission is '*to legislate along The grain of human nature rather than against it*'; thus was The pessimism of Toryism, the presumption humanity is Uniformly self-interested, supremely prone to temptation, Which discounted altruists and philanthropists, martyrs, Saints, and Christians among whom most Tories implausibly Numbered themselves; Toryism depicted itself as '*The political expression of traditional English society... Derived from... 'the tested revelation of British history*"; but Its real triumph was recruiting occasional forward-thinking Figures with semi-progressive reinterpretations of a cynical-Yet-sentimental 'cause' (Joseph Chamberlain among them): '*The master stroke of... Conservatism has been to pre-empt Not merely the nation's past but its national symbols*' – Semiotic alchemy, unsympathetic magic of homegrown Mythology, nostalgia augmented through messaged Legerdemain, mainly by Disraeli, quoted in *The Radical Tory*, 1937: '*The splendour of the Crown... lustre of the peerage... Privileges of the Commons... harmonious union... magnificent Concord of... all classes*' – the Earl of Beaconsfield's '*baroque Imagination*' beguiled British politics for generations...

XIX

Tory prime minister at the time of the Second Reform Bill,
Lord Derby, spun the narrative there was nothing un-Tory in
Extending the franchise to urban working classes, ever self-
Serving the true motive was driven by a visceral survivalism,
To place themselves *'permanently in power,'* as pretend-
Champions of proletarian enfranchisement; John Wilson
Croker's supplemental haunt, the *Quarterly Review*, was
'A bitter critic' of the Second Reform Bill and *'dismissed
The idea of Conservative democracy as a 'phantom.'...
'A vague idea that the poorer men are, the more they are
Influenced by the rich... that the ruder class of minds would
Be more sensitive to traditional emotions'* – that latter trope
Was and still is pivotal to the Tories' magic trick in getting
The working classes to go along with them, the appeal to
'Community, nationalism and pride in Britain's imperial role';
This in turn led to Tories asserting their singular place as
*'The party of the whole nation... uniquely qualified to serve
As... custodians and defenders of British institutions'* – so
The Tories got into the habit of a tub-thumped patriotism to
Appeal to all classes, which set them apart from other parties
As proud protectors of the realm; although Tory prime
Ministers Arthur Balfour and Stanley Baldwin each
Rhetorically acquitted their opponents of tangible intentions
To sabotage the British Empire, their party still *'systematically
And ruthlessly called into question... the patriotism of its
Opponents'* and by doing so *'took its first long step to
Becoming the party... of Imperialism'* – in spite of the Empire
Being seen as more *'a hindrance than... asset to an England
Which saw itself... as 'the workshop of the world' rather than
A latter-day Rome'* (even if it sometimes resembled the latter,
Replete with Roman Air Tube helmets – to morph into foreign
Service pith helmets – worn by British and other European
Troops on colonial campaigns)... McKenzie and Silver made
Mention of Henry Mayhew's *'four remarkable volumes,*
London Labour and the London Poor, *published between
1851 and 1863'* (republished in abridged form as *Mayhew's*

Characters In 1951, edited by Peter Quennell): '*... a rich Picture of life among those who earned... livings on the streets – Costermongers, entertainers... prostitutes. Without sampling Methods... Mayhew... made... forays among these people Recording in minutest detail and in long verbatim extracts*', His '*capacious curiosity... devoted to... firsthand description*', His '*prodigious industry... matched by those later monuments Of research on the urban working class*', Charles Booth's *Life And Labour of the People in London* and Seebohn Rowntree's *Poverty: A Study of Town Life*; almost romantically '*Mayhew Saw the 'street folk' as descendants of 'wandering tribes"* – So-called '*Street Arabs*', while the '*distinctively industrial Working classes lie largely outside his scope*'; Booth and his Peers were '*closer than Mayhew to the working classes Because... they did not view them as belonging to a different Race of men*' and '*did not, like Mayhew, make intrepid sorties In search of the curious, colourful, and exotic*' like some Bowler-hatted – as opposed to pith-helmed – explorers Of Victorian concrete jungles; to McKenzie and Silver writing In the Sixties: "*The problem of understanding the post-war Working class stems not from its poverty but its 'affluence"* And thus the '*contrast between its customary status and... Unprecedented prosperity*'; for their particular study they Sourced working-class voices according to strict criteria: '*Sociologically, the sample was restricted to the 'working Class' – defined as those living in households where the chief Wage earner was employed in a manual occupation... This Definition excludes... those in such marginal occupations as Shop assistant*'; Goldthorpe's groundbreaking paper 'The Affluent Worker and the Thesis of Embourgeoisment', Published in *Sociology*, 1967, proposed the eponymous Concept which described the mostly material uplift of much Of the working class to middle-class levels – in spite of this, At the time McKenzie and Silver were writing, there was '*no Clear and simple connection between relative prosperity and Working class Conservatism*'; as to working-class voting Behaviours, '*A study of Glossop, a small English community*' Suggested '*the existence of long-term political loyalties based*

Upon party commitments... made early in the voting history of Individuals', and Karl Mannhem in *Essays on the Sociology of Knowledge* argued the '*impact of past events can sometimes Be read in the age-profile of an electorate, much as Geological history can be inferred from strata in the earth*'; Where one was placed in the working class had impact on How one voted: '*Upper-working class electors, and those who Think of themselves as middle class, are... more likely to vote Conservative*', greater affluence, opportunities, behavioural Changes, all had an influence: '*Such characteristics... summed Up by the term* embourgeoisment *for which there is no Equivalent in English*'... The deceptive phrase '*the national Interest*' had been rhetorically inculcated in the consciousness Of working-class Tories, invading their vocabulary as McKenzie and Silver found in many respondents:
'*This Unprompted stress by working class Conservatives on The national interest and... personal qualities of leadership is Of great importance*'; McKenzie and Silver recorded verbatim Responses from working class Tories – first on how they Perceived the party: '*They have some of the best brains in The country... They have been brought up to rule... They have No axe to grind for themselves. They look out for... The country as a whole*'; such was the electorally hypnotic Tory mystique which in perceptions of much of the working Classes surrounded the ancient party, aura of entitled Authority – to some '*the Conservatives transcend Partisanship*' and are '*unique custodians of the national Interest*' (that almost magically vague phrase again) and Their '*capacity to govern*' seen as '*of an unmatchable order. Conservatives who are also business leaders are clothed in... Robes of traditional aristocracy*'; counter-intuitively Labour Was seen as '*selfish*', '*greedy*'... '*uneducated*', '*moneyless*'...:
'*Most of them... are out to see what they can gain for Themselves and friends... They haven't the brains to run The country... They are always arguing among themselves*', And '*even when credited with good intentions*' Labour was '*Seen as hampered by incompetence*'; while the Tories, in Spite of being '*out for their own ends*' are '*the only ones you*

Can put in power – you need moneyed... and educated people ... I have nothing against [Labour]. They... have some fine Ideas. They just haven't the capital to back it up' – here it Seemed some working-class perceptions of representative Democracy – through cynicism, naivety, wily insight or Pragmatism – confused it with plutocracy, or at best, Evergetism, assuming government expenditure depended on Private generosity; as to political knowledge and political self-Confidence among working-class voters: *'Inspired... by Marx's concept of the lumpenproletariat, the left has Sometimes thought of working class Conservatives as ill Informed and politically inadequate... The left's task was... to Enlighten them and... integrate them into political life; they Could then be expected to abandon their mistaken behaviour – To develop 'class consciousness"* but Marx's *'concept of The lumpenproletariat'* had been formulated *'in the context of Early industrial society, with its widespread... poverty, and Illiteracy'*, inflammatorily phrased in *The Communist Manifesto*: *'The 'dangerous class,' the social scum, that Passively rotting mass... may... be swept into the movement by A proletarian revolution; its conditions of life, however, Prepare it far more for... a bribed tool of reactionary Intrigue'*; surprisingly McKenzie and Silver found working-Class Tories were *'better informed than Labour voters'*, which Did not *'support the notion'* they were *'victims of political Illiteracy'*, while *'regards Marx's other contention'* that they Were *'alienated from the political process'*, it was found they Were more *'politically confident'* than Labour voters; Working-class views on trades unions were unfavourable: *'They don't want to work these days... They want everything For nothing... The unions have set the people off... People are Happy doing their work; then all of a sudden they think they Want more money'*; such cynical view of unions was as typical Among working-class Labourites as Tories – even when Acknowledging the *'benefits unions confer'* they would Qualify this by adding *'I don't say I hold with the strikes'* or *'They have all these shop stewards... some of them seem to be Communists... they are only stirring up trouble'*; according to

One conflicted shop steward's wife: *'The unions have a lot of Say in... factory life... They must do some good; we wouldn't Have them otherwise. Although I don't believe in them... I Think they take your money and do nothing for you... Them as Got it, won't give it away and they as haven't got it slave away All their lives. But we give for flag days and refugees with Good hearts'* – McKenzie and Silver remarked such political Inconsistencies provided *'a vivid caricature of a pattern that Appears often'*, of unions being seen even by Labourites as Bolshie and *'disruptive'*... Tory propaganda had a slow-drip Effect soaking through working-class consciousness with Soft-soaping, simplistic platitudes and paternalistic pats on The head mopped up in party support, class conflict seen as *'The consequence of... intrusions into mutually beneficial Harmony by radicals, Socialists... those out of sympathy with Traditional British values'* – *'men like Bevan'* who *'made Trouble'*; fingers pointed particularly at more cultured Labourites: *'It is the intellectual, so-called educated type of Man who stirs it up'* – inescapably because the Left wanted to Change society *'the image of 'stirring up conflict' is more Evocative of leftist than of rightist activity'*; it was found The *'rhetoric of class conflict... strikes no... chord among a Large section of the English working class'* – so it seemed, as Still today in the twenty-first century, most of the proletariat Don't appear to want transformational politics that would Benefit them, instead seem intent on sabotaging it, either due To deferential mentality, mass-brainwashing by the right-Wing press, or a combination – above all, have an aversion to Ever being governed by anyone like themselves; it seems The English working classes are their own most remorseless Oppressors, happy accomplices in their own immiseration and Abject cultural lack, enemies of their own long-term interests, Special Constables of self-persecuting inspectorates in paint-Spattered aprons who perceive in relatively impoverished Environments, limited means, depleting spending power, Something agleam with privilege just verging on making Itself visible and graspable at the surface like ancient coinage Gradually emerging from mud and scum under strangely

Alluring magnetic fields of metal detectors; optimists might
See in this a defiant sense of enchantment retained from
Infanthood, lingering glimmerings of magic and imagination –
But it's more tragic and mundane than that: stupidity and
Misplaced aspiration – symbolism and reality are more a case
Of the addictive con of arcade coin pusher machines...

XX

Deferentials seemed to see professions as dynasties: '... *a
Doctor's job... is one's sacrifice of one's life... I think it's got to
Be hereditary'* / '*I feel that especially doctors or dentists... I
Don't think... these people are made – these people are born –
They have to have... instincts for these jobs*' – vocation as
Genetic mystique; deferential attitudes of the Tory portion
Of the proletariat made for pitiful responses but almost as
Depressing was the pessimism of working-class Labourites –
As shown in one respondent seemingly expressing what
Marx Termed *entfremdung* (*estrangement*) from the '*species-
Essence*' (*Gattungswesen*), alienation of labour under
Capitalism: '*You don't see anything that exists; you only get
A verdict of some kind. No, I'd like to see something produced
... something with labour*', as opposed to factory mass-
Production of useless commodities; but from the same
Respondent there was also deferential self-defeatism: '*You
Don't get anywhere now without some sort of certificate*' but
'*They get too snobbish if they go to school too long*' – verdict:
'*... parental ambition for children is... circumscribed by...
Class-bound horizons*'... The '*elite symbols*' of the House
Of Lords and monarchy, historically associated with
The Conservative party, a perception it exploited efficaciously
Among working-class '*subjects of the realm*' who showed '*few
Expressions of... abolitionist sentiment*' – conscientious
'*Subjects*' as opposed to conscious citizens; similar responses
Came when same questions were asked in Eric Nordlinger's
Working Class Tories (1969): '*... large proportions of English*

Working class voters are prone to support the Conservatives
As the party of their natural social superiors who are... better
Equipped to govern than men who have risen from
The working class'; asked to pick a hypothetical prime
Minister either from a similar background to theirs, or plucked
From social elites, Tory-supporting informants placed
Importance on '*breeding*' and '*superior education*': '*I think*
The son of an M.P. is educated deep down, more than
The ordinary working class man', this kind of '*deferential*
Response' was also found in some Labour-supporting
Respondents, and so '*deference in itself*' was not a '*sovereign*
Explanation' for working-class Toryism; thus McKenzie and
Silver identified '*two distinct types*' of working-class Tories:
'*Deferential*', and '*non-deferential*' or '*secular*', a term '*used in*
A metaphoric sense'; deferentials tended to '*invest...*
Conservative leaders with... transcendent superiority over all
... political rivals which borders on the magical' (in spite
Of two distinct types identified, this was no Procrustean
Approach, since some informants were classed as 'mixed' –
Respondents were interviewed in four phases, the fourth,
Conducted October 1963, coincided with the 'Profumo affair'
To which most respondents seemed sanguine, even
Sympathetic to the point of apologism for the minister's
Indiscretions, because it made him seem '*more human*' – just
As rampant philandering and unexplained children made
Rabelaisian 'Boris' all the more lovable to a public who
Rewarded him with a thumping majority); '*Deferentials prefer*
Leaders of socially superior origins who, they assume, will
Have inherited capacities for leadership'; any policies
Benefiting ordinary people were perceived by them '*as...*
Consequence of... generosity and benevolence or... personal
Wealth of politicians of elite origins' – euergetism;
Deferentials accepted '*the monarchy and... Lords as...*
Essential symbols of British... nationhood' – the subservient
View: '*I took to my Queen very highly. Nothing... needs to be*
Improved... To many [the monarchy] *should come to a*
Common level. If they did, they wouldn't be Monarchy';
The Tory party was seen as '*a national institution different*

In kind from... other parties: 'There's... background which
Counts... The qualities to make a Prime Minister are in
The breeding" – most responses, contradictory, anacoluthon,
Nonsensical, nonsequitous: *'It's something... ingrained in*
Them. He's been to a good public school and I know a lot of
People run them down [but] *you can tell breeding*'; secular
Conservatives looked more at the forward thrust of
Tory Policies, the *'getting things done'* pragmatics: *'They're... for*
Free enterprise... Things are not left to stagnate, they are
Progressive... the H-Bomb, Labour wants to give it up' –
'Progressiveness' in their eyes, then, meant more effective
Means of blowing ourselves up; *'They... are not for*
The working man, but... we are better off than when Labour is
In power. They do treat us well' / 'If you haven't got money it's
No good; so you have got to go to the party with capital' /
'... if you mix with money you can gain some... When
The Labour got in, the Conservatives froze the money. It
Makes unemployment': an implicit assumption evergetism is
At the heart of right-wing government and may *'be withdrawn*
At the will of the elite'; but *'far from engendering hostility'* it
Encouraged greater deference; time and again responses
Implied perception of the party as custodians of patriotism,
Holding a *'special symbolic national status: 'I am a true blue.*
It's a case of my country right or wrong... The party knows
More than I do, and I trust them...' / 'Half these Labour boys
Don't give tuppence for the country. The Conservatives
Encourage you to act fair, poor and rich alike... They... treat
Everyone the same' – just not equally; over and over
The Conservative Party perceived as a unifying force for
The country; *'Every man at heart is a capitalist... you go for*
The money and... brains. Either you feel Tory or you don't...
Any thinking man votes Tory. They have something that's
Traditional'... While conceding *'Conservative voters are in*
No sense a lumpenproletariat when compared with Labour
Voters', McKenzie and Silver asked whether the deferentials
Among them were lumpen, at least in self-perception, since
They perceived class as caste: *'Breeding decides it, which can*
Only be gained after generations... Education and money

Don't give breeding'; on whether this state of affairs was fair:
'*Well, you... go back to the old hymn, 'All Things Bright and
Beautiful... God Gave them High and Low*'; more disturbing
And surprising: '*Some Labour voters... share the essentially
Deferential view that class is immutably determined by birth*';
Deferentials were keep-in-their-place traditionalists, seculars,
Apprentice capitalists; deferentials were chary of VAT: '*If I
Was making laws I'd put more on luxuries, such as television
... but I think it would be a good idea to take a little bit off
Tobacco*' – the poor man's luxury (though also that
Of the struggling shabby-genteel writer, as George Orwell,
Who tustled with the problem of books and tobacco in his
1946 essay 'Books vs. Cigarettes': '*With prices as they now
Are, I am spending far more on tobacco than... on books
('Penguins and other cheap editions'). I smoke six ounces a
Week, at half-a-crown an ounce, making nearly £40 a year*
[Which] *would just about pay for a packet of Woodbines
Every day*'); deferentials were intransigently loyal to party,
A hereditary loyalty: '*I am a Conservative. My father was
Conservative. He was a working man... even when he'd got
Nothing, he... voted Conservative.' / 'The Conservatives... are
Gentry. They know how to behave. I believe in them*'; seculars'
Loyalty was more conditional: '*You are all the time between
Two evils and you choose the lesser of the two*' (confessions
Echoed over fifty years later by 'red wall' Tory voters);
Deferentials' antipathy towards Labour was self-defeating:
'*... They are always promising people something... I don't think
They can fulfil... Because nothing has happened to convince
Me they know anything about governing a country*'... At
The time of this research the trend of working-class Toryism
Was from deference to secularism; this would later mutate
Into Thatcherism, beyond that, merge with a new deference
To Etonian Toryism, and resurgent Monarchism, mingled
With Thatcherite property-worship, one-upmanship –
A travesty of traits; deferentials felt the Tories were '*qualified
To manage scarce resources: '... they have rallied the country
Round and we're more prosperous now... Mr. Wilson is telling
Us... when* [Labour] *get in it's gonna be all right... but they*

Can't do the impossible... You'd run the country dry... But a Lot of people take that bait'; deference fuelled most working-Class Toryism bolstered by *'display of symbols and status... Not merely a vestige of... past... aristocratic hegemony'*, but its Liver, self-regenerating... In their final chapter, 'Retrospect And Prospect', McKenzie and Silver drew conclusions:
'A century has passed since the debate over... enfranchisement Of the working class... The expectations of... Socialists and Conservatives about the behaviour of working class voters Have been denied by events. The Socialist vision... of an Increasingly... class-conscious working class, fundamentally Hostile to... capitalistic society, has not been fulfilled. Neither Have the apprehensions of... Conservatives' whose *'long-term Domination of British governments since the late nineteenth Century'* has been down to *'half... of its votes'* coming from The *'manual working class'*; as for what Bagehot the weeping Prophet foretold in the 1860s – *"deference,' the supply of Which... seemed even larger than that of the coal below The surface of England, is dwindling... since the Industrial Revolution'* – the seam proved far more plentiful and self-Replenishing than presumed, a vast coalface of deference; *'Thus Marx the social revolutionary and Bagehot The 'hesitating Gladstonian'... had... to revise these Expectations. Marx early discerned the profound social Conservatism of the English working class'*; far from simply Relying on deference Tory leaders made Disraelian Adaptations to policy and thereby tempted proletarian electors With *'material benefits and social improvements'*, a *'twofold Appeal'* helped by the fact that *'uniquely in Britain, among Western democracies, symbols of social hierarchy are fused With those of national loyalty and sovereignty. By pre-Empting traditional symbols'* the Tories lifted themselves *'Above the swirl of political struggle'* and avoided *'a purely Material competition for working class votes than which Bagehot could 'conceive of nothing more corrupting... for a Set of poor ignorant people"*; the Tories also had the distinct Advantage of not being *'constrained by... programmatic Doctrine – whether Manchester Liberalism or Socialism'* thus

'Freer to compete... opportunistically' in the *'political market'*;
What was clear was the working classes were less polarised
Than British politics was polarising in being *'dominated by
Two major parties'* which imposed *'a dichotomous choice
Upon the working class electorate... many of whom share
Fundamental attitudes... Politics is not a source of deep
Cleavage in British society. Working class people who vote
Differently are not... sharply different'* in other respects:
The perception of the Conservative party *'as necessary to hold
The balance between competing interests, to regulate conflict'* –
Still more implausibly from a post-Thatcherite vantage – *'to
Rebuke greed (whether of capital or Labour)'*, hence in effect
Be referees, remained, up until the Eighties; for further
Advantage to the Tories, blue collar Labourites were quicker
To *'acknowledge... shortcomings of the party they support'*
Than were true blue collars, and were also critical of the trade
Unions, reflecting *'impact of... newspaper comment to which
The working class is exposed (both in Conservative... papers
And in the moderately left Press like the* Daily Mirror*)'*;
Working-class Tories viewed their own class as *'a source of...
Greedy demands which threaten the delicate balance... of
Society'*; working-class Labourites were more electorally
Conflicted, often feeling they had to *'choose between class
Interests... and a party'* they saw as *'more competent and
National'*; deferentials believed the *'material interests of
Ordinary people'* were *'best advanced by entrusting... a
Delicate economy to those... uniquely qualified to manage
These esoteric matters'*, Labour was *'credited with good
Intentions but condemned as intrusive and incompetent'*; in
Spite of being the most industrialised country in Europe with
A high rate of political literacy, Britain was still steeped in
Deference – a very British pestilence: although *'rising levels
Of education and the spread of non-religious culture... can...
Weaken the sense of deference* [they] *do so in England more
Slowly... The extent to which national symbols are drawn
From... the privileged elite has meant... identifying oneself as
British promoted... deference'* – no semiotic reckoning in
The United Kingdom as happened across Europe: *'The advent*

Of modern politics in many European nations required
The rejection of traditional symbols... but in Britain...
Integration of the new working classes into the national
Community involved... acceptance of these symbols'; precisely
Because *'English institutions and values were more modern*
Than those of other European societies in the pre-industrial
Phase' they underwent *'fewer disruptive changes'*; and unlike
Most European nations where sovereignty is invested in
'The people', *'in Britain it is the Crown in Parliament that is*
Sovereign' and *'assigns to ordinary people the role, not of*
Citizens, but... subjects' thus serving *'to promulgate...*
Doctrines... which have continued to nourish working class
Conservatism'... So we are belatedly learning the working
Classes, who it was always thought would be mobilised in
The cause of Socialism, are its biggest obstacles, persistent
Self-persecutors, flummoxed corporals instructing themselves
With ventriloquised orders, spontaneous conscripts propping
Up their oppressors at expense of their own emancipation,
Unadulterated Ragged Trousered Philanthropists –
Detrimentally, Robert Tressell's epochal tome was not as
Ubiquitous on working-class bookshelves as some believed,
Although copies were lapped up by anxious corporals and
Rankers in the army in and after the Second World War,
A reach of readership thought to have contributed to Labour's
Landslide in '45 almost as much as its manifesto;
The literatures digested by the British proletariat were
Of varied flavourings and adulterated ingredients...

{Self-improvement used to be a pastime of the proles –
O whatever happened to all those anxious corporals?}

XXI

Ken Worpole's *Dockers and Detectives: Popular Reading, Popular Writing*, published 1983, groundbreaking in
Salvaging for posterity obscured, neglected or forgotten
British proletarian literature and reading habits of the 1930s
And 40s, an entire shadow-culture criminally discarded:
'The fragmentation of working class... cultural consciousness
Now fiercely debated by... such writers as Eric Hobsbawm, Stuart
Hall, and... Jeremy Seabrook, is not... surprising given
The fragmentation [of] material artefacts of that
Consciousness... allowed to disappear through neglect, or...
Killed at the roots by recurring frosts of socialist economism.
The banners were allowed to go mouldy'; history, even
Proletarian, distrusted by socialists more interested in future
Narratives; *'Such processes were not actively resisted, yet*
People are surprised that 'consciousness' has become
'Discontinuous"; Worpole praised *'the development of non-*
Commercial local publishing in Britain' which had *'created...*
Large numbers of new readers for forms of writing...
Conventionally felt... [to be] *coterie interests, such as poetry'*;
Worpole stripped down popular culture, its self-perpetuating
Confected rhetoric pretending choice, central to capitalism
And commercial culture when in fact the system mostly made
The choice on behalf of consumers: *'What people* want to read
And what they are able to buy *are two separate things though*
... as long as... cultural production... remains part of...
Capitalist production we cannot... get the range of literature
And history that a cultural democracy would expect';
Capitalism had a distanced relationship to readerships *'other*
Than that of the cash nexus. One lesson we ought to learn
From the 1930s is... [how] *the working class... responded to*
The inability of capitalist cultural production to meet felt
Needs by developing its own film-making, theatre-making,
Photographic and documentary recording projects as well as
Socialist publishing initiatives' – in his own time, Worpole
Was at the forefront of a similar movement of mutual
Improvement and cultural exchange through the Hackney

Writers Workshop which produced the groundbreaking
Anthology *Where There's Smoke*, 1984; capitalist publishing
Attempted to absorb countercultural activity, swallow up
Radical writing but, crucially, while it might publish such
Output, it could not *'create these literatures, only'* – like
Monopolistic moths – *'hover around the movements which...*
Create them and try to buy these texts second-hand', this was
'The pattern of... capitalist intellectual production' as
Described by Hans Magnus Enzensberger: *'The mind industry*
Can take on anything, digest it, reproduce, and pour it out.
Whatever our minds can conceive of is grist to its mill...
It is capable of turning any idea into a slogan... any work of
The imagination into a hit. This is its overwhelming power,
Yet... also its most vulnerable spot: it thrives on [that] *which it*
Cannot manufacture by itself... depends on the very substance
It must fear most, and must suppress what it feeds on:
The creative productivity of the people'; hence a parasitic
Culture of awards and prizes, talent scouts, literary agents,
Eye-watering advances that pit poets, writers and artists
Against one another in a cattle market of creativity-enervating
Competitiveness... Worpole noted that the English novel had
Originated in *'criminal ballads and the street literature of*
London's underworld or demi-monde... *Until the Stamp Act,*
Most broadsheet... publications hardly ever distinguished...
Factual from... fictional; what are wholly distinct categories
Of writing for us today were then part of a single literary
Discourse' (although the tabloids have kept up the tradition
Of 'fictfact'); the Stamp Act *'forced publishers to distinguish*
The two since [it] *put a tax on news and left all other forms of*
Writing untaxed. Yet... ambiguity about the reality of what is
Told in fictional writing... remains with us... connected to
[the] almost mesmeric quality of the printed word'... AE
Dobbs recalled a Grassington miner, *'collector of chap-books,*
Who believed what he read. 'It is not likely,' he argued,
'... Anyone would go to the expense of printing lies" – a naivety
On which to this day red top newspaper circulation relies;
19th century radical publisher Richard Carlile asserted he was
An implacable enemy of all fiction... Everything of this kind

Should... go into the fire. He who burns a romance purifies
The human mind' – might have bubbled from the censorial
Mouth of the fanatical Fire Captain in *Fahrenheit 451* in
Which all literature is burnt, the printed word verboten, only
Pictures permitted, comic strips without speech-bubbles,
'Parlor walls' transmitting asinine reality entertainments, not
Unlike 21st c. plasma screens... Worpole examined working-
Class reading habits: *'One of the great strengths of the British*
Working-class socialist movement has been its keen interest in
Literature and other... imaginative writing. The general
Studies of the 19th century working class reading public...
Those of Altick, Wickwar, Webb, James, Neuberg and Simons
Continually attest to this... Then there is Engel's memorable
Famous passage in The Condition of the English Working
Class' which depicts the autodidact: *'I have often heard*
Working-men, whose fustian jackets scarcely hold together,
Speak upon... subjects, with more knowledge than most
'Cultivated' bourgeois in Germany possess'; yet proletarian
Literary talents could find fertile ground in which to root,
Even in coarser literatures, cultivating themselves on
Whichever weeds, scrub or primitive plants they could gather,
Great trees could grow from humblest shrubs, and blossom, as
Worpole noted, literate tastes and voracious verbal appetites
Could be nourished on scraps of scantiest nutrition: *'The early*
19th-century radical Samuel Bamford was from an early age
Intoxicated by the lurid chap-book stories he found... in
A local printer's shop'; yet the best diet for working-class
Readers had been in proletarian literature itself: *'Mary Ashraf's...*
Introduction to Working Class Literature in Great
Britain *details the... history of the fictional promotion of*
Challenging ideas from the Chartist novels of Ernest Jones,
GWM Reynolds and Thomas Frost through... trade union
Novels of the 1870s... up to Tressell's The Ragged Trousered
Philanthropists *and the novels of Ethel Carnie... In the 1930s*
Such writers as Howard Fast and Frank Tilsley managed to
Be both popular and political, but since the Second World
War there has been little attempt by socialists to use fictional
Means to present oppositional ideas'; Worpole pointed out

The importance of acknowledging that *'working-class reading Patterns have often been... more... internationalist than... Patterns of middle-class reading'*, particularly amongst Autodidacts; Worpole cited post-war European and International reading trends amongst working-class readers Who lapped up Camus, Sartre, de Beauvoir, Grass, Bradbury, Brautigan, Mailer, Salinger, Trocchi, Lowry, Moorcock: *'... The existence of Penguin Books was of real material Importance in encouraging... interest... in European and American writing in the 1960s'* – Worpole noted of his time: *'Even today working-class people with only secondary school Education remain numerically the largest reading public in Britain, and... possibly the most eclectic and radical'* – Something tragically broken up by the plough blades of that Thatcheritic decade; Worpole acknowledged the *'difficulties In talking about the many... variegated traditions of working-Class writing in Britain'* in 'the *long shadow cast by Robert Tressell's* The Ragged Trousered Philanthropists, *first Published in 1914* [posthumously, four years after it was Completed and submitted to publishers (who returned The manuscript unread because it wasn't typed), even then, Abridged and bowdlerised under patronage of patriotic *Daily Express* poet Jessie Pope, gutted of its core socialist message By Grant Richards Ltd., only to be reconstructed unabridged And with its original ending intact, belatedly, in 1955, never Since out of print...]... *and still dominating many discussions About early socialist culture'* – one of the most striking things About this novel-cum-polemic, its critical depiction of urban Working-class painter-decorators as complicit in their own Oppression through lapping up confected petty politics, Celebrity- and royalty-saturated trivialities and anti-socialist Propaganda of Tory-supporting newspapers, frustrations just About sated by a diet of adulterated tea, beer and cheap Cigarettes, ultimately deaf to attempts at Marxist education by The only Socialist among them, Frank Owen, resistant to his Doses of class-consciousness; Worpole remarked through his Own experiences in socialist politics over many years he had *'Met a number of people for whom the problem of socialist*

Culture would be solved by the arrival of an updated sequel to Tressell's book' – but in its absence, Worpole celebrated *'Contemporary movements in adult literacy, people's history, And... resurgence of working class writing through workshops And local publishing projects'* which had *'created a... new Kind of oppositional cultural and educational politic'* – here Worpole pinpointed the sublime bouleversement of socialist Cultural exchange: *'... whereas earlier working-class adult Educational Movements in Britain... such as the National Council of Labour Colleges and the Workers' Educational Association, were strongly predicated on... what it was Assumed people* didn't know, *on their 'ignorance', these new Forms of cultural struggle are based much more... radically On what people* do know... *The 'rediscovery' of adult Illiteracy in Britain in the early 1970s... unleashed a Tremendously liberating debate on the meaning of 'literacy"*, That *'the ability to read was not enough and... opportunities For writing had to be included in any fully formed definition Of cultural literacy'*, and as a result of this small, local but Radical educational recalibration the *'Ruskin College-inspired History Workshop Movement, and... network of working-class Writers' workshops... affiliated to the Federation of Worker Writers and Community Publishers, have... been based on a Generic commitment to people's own cultural productivity'*... Worpole noted *'radical and Marxist traditions of... cultural Criticism have been no more sympathetic to... possibilities of Popular literature'* than *'belles-lettristic'* and *'Leavisite Academic criticisms... Socialist criticism has also failed to... Acknowledge... new narrative developments'*; detective fiction Originally took a radical form in William Godwin's *Caleb Williams or Things As They Are* (1794): *'... the murder [and] Its... ramifications were... a device around which a political Critique of prevailing economic and social relationships Could be assembled'* (that last decade of the eighteenth Century also witnessed the *'establishment'* and *'rapid Suppression'* of the *'first working-class political organisation'*, The London Corresponding Society); such radicalism under Cover of detective fiction however was to be shadowed in

The dawn of *'the era of the great gentlemen-detectives'* –
Poe's Dupin, Margery Allingham's Campion, HC McNeile's
'Bulldog' Drummond, Agatha Christie's Poirot – which made
'The genre... the perfect fictional form for the sacramentality
Of... executive institutions'; but there remained sub-textual
Layers to detective fiction: *'Carlo Ginzburg... outlined a*
Detailed analogy between principles of crime detection as
Exemplified by Conan Doyle's Sherlock Holmes and... near
Contemporaneous principles of art detection as formulated by
Giovanni Morelli and the observations of Freud in
The Psychopathology of Everyday Life. *All three 'detectives'*
Were developing theories based on the belief... it was in
The seemingly insignificant gestures and details of human
Behaviour... the real clues to... personality were to be found' –
And what was psychology but principles of detection applied
To personalities, prejudices, beliefs, foibles, consciousness
And the unconscious (there'd even been a fictional fusion
Of these associations in Nicholas Meyer's *The Seven-Per-Cent*
Solution (1974) in which Sherlock Holmes visits Sigmund
Freud in Vienna to undergo hypnosis to cure his cocaine
Addiction and associated delusions); *'Apart from a...*
Glorification of British imperialism', these novels tended to
Portray *'the working class as an atavistic mob battering down*
The park railings'; and the prose grew more and more
Masculine – on the theme of the *'masculine style'* in popular
Fiction, chiefly of the detective novel, Worpole expressed
Disagreement with Hoggart's take in *The Uses of Literacy*:
'[Hoggart] *was right to see... the prose style itself as*
Something new – vernacular... tough – though in describing it
As 'debased Hemingway'... failed to consider that
Hemingway's... unrhetorical, unsentimental style' developed
Parallel to that of *'dime magazine writer'* Dashiell Hammett;
By contrast, most *'British novelists... resisted modernising*
Developments in narration and style' and *'even when socialist*
Writers' such as C Day Lewis, GDH and Margaret Cole,
And Christopher Caudwell wrote genre fiction, they failed to
Use it *'as a medium for any accompanying radical...*
Technique or ideas, but... let the genre determine the form...

Almost completely'; even within this occasionally destructive
'*Masculine style*' of writing further cultural change was
Brewing in Britain by the late Fifties, a rupture of working-
Class literary talents in the '*Kitchen Sink*'/'*Angry Young
Man*' insurgency – a raft of novels and plays depicting
Proletarian antiheroes piling one on the other in rapid demotic
Decoupage: Keith Waterhouse's *Billy Liar*, Brendan Behan's
Bortsal Boy, Alan Sillitoe's Arthur Seaton (*Saturday Night
And Sunday Morning*), John Braine's social Climber Joe
Lampton (*Room At the Top*), John Osborne's raging graduate
Market-stall trader Jimmy Porter (*Look Back in Anger*), Stan
Barstow's white collar Vic Brown (*A Kind of Loving*)...

XXII

On 'Popular Literature of the Second World War' Worpole
Noted while the literature of the first was extensively
Documented, literary critics had dismissed much literature
Of the Second, that from the ranks – save for the poetry
Of a select clutch of university-educated talents including
Oxbridge's Sidney Keyes, Keith Douglas, Hamish Henderson,
And Redbrickers Henry Reed and Alun Lewis (Keyes,
Douglas and Lewis all fatalities of the war), all officer class,
Who '*in poetry are mentioned as constituting a small
Qualification that prevents the complete dismissal of
The literature of the 1939–1945 period*' – but what
Of the writings of '*the other ranks*''? Worpole called this a
'*Cultural myopia of English literary criticism... The barbed
Wire fence... which separates 'literature' from 'writing'... it is
Whole literatures and cultural processes, social relationships
Of reading, writing and publishing, which... if dismissed,
Could leave the social activities of reading and writing (that
Is to say, literature) ineluctably at the whim of market forces*';
Worpole pinpointed two exceptional '*novels about
The experiences of combatants*', Alexander Baron's *From
The City, From the Plough* (1948) and Dan Billany's *The Trap*

(1950), *'both written by working-class socialists'* – but such
Striking work was given scant attention compared to more
Tepid potboilers, patriotic bestsellers focusing on mass escape
Attempts from POW camps *'which promoted a notion of
'Freedom'... abstract and talismanic'* that contaminated
The mainstream war narratives with *'the vocabulary of
Conservatism as a rallying call against... communitarian...
Mutual association'*; most bestselling war novelists' depictions
Of life back home in Britain were bucolic rather than urbanic,
One might think when reading HE Bates *'the Britain of
Unemployment, large urban slums, rickets, TB, Relieving
Officers, tied cottages... and... other manifestations of a
Deeply divided class society, simply didn't exist'*; Bates
Depicted RAF pilots as sky bound Elizabethans *'adventuring
In the air, as the great navigators had'* the seas; England
Of such green dreamers *'evoked by... mythology of Agincourt
And rural Arcadia of* A Midsummer Night's Dream... *one of
Robust yeomanry, rustic sensuality and courtly love'*, which
Prompted Worpole to make a contemporary polemical point:
*'In complete contrast, the Conservative Government under
Margaret Thatcher would rather invoke the... mercantile
Values of Victorian economic rapaciousness'* – a profiteering
Puritanism; Worpole opined: *'What can radicalism offer
Compared with ... imagery of long Edwardian summers,
Streets swept clean by deferential working men... and Britain
Once again a world power?'* – the pulling power of Empire;
What was *'one of the great strengths of the socialist cause –...
An appeal to a New Golden Age – has foundered in... post-
Industrial society'* while the popular imagination had been
Easily drawn by the warm glow of nostalgia; *'The vision of
The socialist revival of the 1870s onwards, exemplified in Robert
Blatchford's* Merrie England *and in Walter Crane's
Garlanded figures bringing the harvest home, or dancing
Round the May-Pole'* (as well as in Ruskin's writings, the Pre-
Raphaelites' art, and Morris's Arts and Crafts Movement) was
Another kind of nostalgia, *'an appeal to return to a lost
Commonwealth, an agricultural past... disappeared. Without
A... vision of things as they could be, it is not surprising...*

People will want to revert to things as they were. Because...
The present is always unbearable to everybody. Labourism
Never comes to terms with this crucial problem'; simultaneous
To this migration back in time to more rustic culture –
Ancestral Arcadia – of artisan crafts, handmade objects and
Furniture, the view that there was much the contemporary
Metropolitan chattering classes could learn from carpentered
Simplicity of rural folk of yesteryear, amid a tacit '*late-*
Victorian revolt' in the Yellow Nineties (Mauve Decade to
Americans), scraping tectonic plates of the *fin-de-siecle*, was
The first patroned attempt to culturally educate one
Of the more promising minds of labouring classes through
The transformational auspices of Ruskin College, Oxford,
Founded in the final year of that decade, which opened up
The wood-panelled dorms – former hallowed grounds
Of younger privileged – to working-class scholars, sundry
Jude the Obscures (only four years after Hardy's tragedy was
Thrown like a clanging gauntlet into the public realm
Of opprobrium, taboo and moral horror – rather than, as his
Wife would have preferred, onto a fire), with no formal
Qualifications but obvious aptitude '*to educate themselves*
Efficiently at nominal cost', either to attend the ancient halls
Of learning, or pursue correspondence courses (in spite
Of '*economic pressure to add to... family income as soon as*
Possible' which Ruskin's Vice-Principal claimed still dogged
Many students) – this nascent Mecca of academic access for
Self-improving proletarian pilgrims established by two
Americans, Charles A Beard and Walter Vrooman, funded by
Vrooman's wife Anne (née Grafflin), in many respects
The concrete precursor to Pelican and the Open University
Through which armies of self-improving corporals trooped...
Worpole honed in on dissenting postwar writers: Alexander
Baron, demobbed 1946, wrote *From The City, From The*
Plough '*at nights*', something he felt compelled to write
'*Because after the war the first few novels to get published*
Were all by officers, or by the kind of intellectuals to whom
The army was an agony' – those 'gentlemen rankers' and
'Anxious corporals' – Worpole: '*The values that emanate*

From Baron's book are not those of some mythologised
'England' or specious nationalism' – patchwork patriotism –
'But of a class that puts the welfare of others, mutual support
And solidarity, above the values of individualism; Dan
Billany *'attended some classes for unemployed young people and*
Went on to... Hull University', he spent the third chapter of his
Novel *The Trap* in diatribe: *'It used to be the fashion to see*
The working class from a little distance – if not through bars
... through an impervious psychological screen' whose lives
Were seen as irrelevant *'as those of flatfish on the floor of*
The aquarium, on the other side of... thick glass... in their own
Bottlegreen element... As examples of Humble Worth,
The working class at one time challenged the dog'; yet
Apolitical depictions of the war dominated the mainstream,
Monopolised readerships and helped shape an incipient post-
War patriotism and nostalgia for a golden England of green
Legend – the Churchillian giant would wrestle with
The Attleean titan, the unionist lion with the socialist unicorn:
'The political climate of the early 1950s was becoming rapidly
Different from... 1945. Then, there had been an air of radical
Change... of going forward to an alternative society. Yet with
The return of a Conservative Government in 1951, after a
Long period of Labour rationing and austerity, the political
Atmosphere was already in retreat... A war... fought in
The name of anti-Fascism... was by then already... being
Reconstructed as a war to preserve the old order'... Worpole
Swooped back to the 1930s as the last fertile period for radical
British proletarian literature noting *'recent attention to*
The writing of that decade' hasn't yet acknowledged *'attempts*
To create a different aesthetic of working-class experience'
Rooted in rootlessness, *'dislocation and transience'*, the most-
Remembered working-class writers of the 1930s had depicted
'Communities they lived in', titles and writers such as *Means*
Test Man by Walter Brierley, *These Poor Hands* by BL Combes,
Cwymardy and *We Live* By Lewis Jones, *May Day* by
John Sommerfield (not to mention *Shabby Tiger* by
Howard Spring, and *The Stars Look Down* and *The Citadel* by –
The albeit more middle class – AJ Cronin, books strikingly

Jacketed in Gollancz' maize yellow hardback range), *'literary Documents rooted in... class... place'* and *'local industry'*; and In this documenting of *'pit villages and industrial towns of... 'Unknown England''* they were *'encouraged by... developing Oppositional aesthetics of that period. The poetry of Auden, Spender, C-Day Lewis and MacNiece explored the imagery of The derelict Industrial North'* – the 'Pylon Poets' scouted out From 'Auden Country' to explore contemporary developments Impinging on picturesque countryside, as one of their crop, Stanley Snaith, put it hauntingly in his poem 'Pylons':

> *...outposts of the trekking future.*
> *Into the thatch-hung consciousness of hamlets*
> *They blaze new thoughts, new habits. Traditions*
> *Are being trod down like flowers dropped by children.*
> *Already that farm-boy striding and throwing seed*
> *In the shoulder-hinged half-circle Millet knew,*
> *Looks grey with antiquity as his dead forbears,*
> *A half familiar figure out of the Georgics,*
> *Unheeded by these new-world, rational towers...*

Similarly to Richard Hoggart before him Worpole focused On anomic working-class talents *'for whom class was Experienced as... dislocation... rootlessness... constant search For employment – often involving moving from town to town. There was also... extreme psychological isolation'* – such Experiences were depicted in the novels of George Garrett, James Hanley and Jim Phelan, all Liverpool-Irish writers Of the Twenties and Thirties, Scousers Obscure who between Them developed a *'different tradition of... 'proletarian' Literature'* concerned with displacement *'from settled... Communities'*; like most *'unknown working-class writers'* they Were only able to get published with help from left-wing Luminaries... James Hanley *'was born in 1901 in a Merseyside Catholic family and went to sea at... fourteen'*, After nine years he *'settled with the idea of becoming a writer'* – Not unlike Jack London's eponymous sailor turned writer in *Martin Eden*; Hanley's Expressionist depictions of Liverpool

Slum life evoked Edvard Munch, Malcolm Lowry, and LS
Lowry; in his debut novel, *Drift* (1930) Hanley was depicted
'Socialist politics' through gritted proletarian lens as spiced
With hypocrisy and pretention represented by *'middle and
Upper-class aesthetes who lounge about in each other's flats
Listening to Beethoven and talking about Tolstoy and modern
Sculpture'* – scarf-twirlers of the Knowledge District; his
Follow-up novel, *Boy* (1931), shocked more sensibilities and
'Went through three... rapid reprints' before being *'banned for
Obscenity in 1932'* – never to be republished; it took to task
Toxic working-class masculinity at its most brutalising –
A *Sturm und Drang Bildungsroman* in the vein of Goethe's
Sorrows of Young Werther or Musil's *The Confusions of
Young Törless*; Hanley was fascinated by *'the supposedly
'Inarticulate', whose inner minds are... endless seas'*, such was
His boundless belief in potential of all human minds, and
The least articulated of these all the more intriguing for
Unarticulated secrecies – Noble Savages of urban England;
Jim Phelan's best known work was *Ten-A-Penny-People*
(1938), in it, the young protagonist *'is taken on board ship
Where he is... befriended by an older sailor known as 'Soshie'
(The Socialist) who gives him a volume of Jack London stories'*,
Phelan is critical of *'the politically rigid as in his
Portrayal of one Communist couple who can only... speak in
Truncated phrases like modern Gradgrinds'* [...or like
The compact-speak in Nigel Kneale's *The Year of the Sex
Olympics* (1968), a comment on postmodernist apathy
Depicting a future dystopia of passive receptiveness among
A populace sensorily doped by constant streams of sports and
Pornography fused into one onanistic entertainment medium,
A play which predicted the advent of reality television – and
In many respects a depiction of Richard Hoggart's worst
Nightmare, all-consuming consumerism, and in decades we'd
Be halfway there with the Bazalgette revolution in tele-
Voyeurism]... The Liverpool-Irish writers were steeped in
The salty tradition of *'Ibsen, Strindberg, Synge, Joyce,
Gorky... Dostoevsky, Faulkner... Jack London's* Sea Wolf,
Conrad Aitken's Blue Voyage, *Malcolm Lowry's* Ultramarine,

O'Neill's The Hairy Ape' and Melville and Conrad who *'had*
Explored this world of harrowing... voyages' allegorically...
Maritime travels were perfect settings, destructive elemental
Immersions, to study themes of the fluid and mutable – what
Emile Durkheim in *Suicide* (1897) termed *'anomie'* –
'Displacement, fragmentariness, cosmopolitanism', life adrift
On the streets... Worpole philosophised: *'one of the paradoxes*
Of writing – particularly for working-class people' was that
'At the same time as many... acquire their first typewriter, they
Also acquire their first suitcase' and then feel compelled to
'Remove themselves in order to write: to... a particular
District... known to be a place for 'writing' – Grub Street,
Bloomsbury, Soho, Hampstead'; in Simon Blumenfield's *Jew Boy*
(1935), the protagonist Alec visits an *'old school friend*
Who has moved out into the suburbs' and is now one
Of the *'progressive'* middle class – there's a powerful moment
When *'left on his own'* Alec *'surveys the bookshelves:*
'Warwick Deeping, Ethel Mannin, David Garnett, Arthur
Symons. Several Shakespeares... a Dickens set... Bernard
Shaw... HG Wells... a fat Nuttall's Dictionary... You only had
To pick up one of these books, and your mind soared into
The vast empyrean, and you forgot there were such... things...
As unemployment... and... slums'; Joe Jacobs' account of his
Time as a member of the Stepney Young Communist League
Describes a reading list in the manner of one building up
Their drugs stamina: *'It started with...* The Ragged Trousered
Philanthropists, *through to... Upton Sinclair, Jack London,*
John Dos Passos, Romain Rolland, Mann, Remarque, Ibanez,
Tolstoy, Gorky... William Morris, Robert Owen, HG Wells,
Arnold Bennett, JB Priestley. Then there was the heavy
Stuff... Marx... in pamphlet form – Value, Price and Profit;
Wage Labour... *Eventually, we went on to tackle* Capital'...
Willie Goldman's *East End My Cradle* captured life in
'The garment industry, or 'Rag trade' – Worpole remarked
Goldman was the best documenter of the *'cultural faultline...*
Between the working-class writer and the communal culture
Which becomes the subject of the writing. For though
The writers might see themselves as chroniclers' or

'Folklorists' those they wrote about could come to see them as
*'Informers, collaborators... spies..: 'People with warped lives
Will forgive you anything but being different from themselves'*;
Another of Goldman's stories returns to this theme: *'... They
Claim, proudly, that I, who am a 'writer', have brought
The family tradition of loafing to its logical conclusion"* –
Recalling how Jack London's eponymous protagonist in
Martin Eden (1909), a navvy turned struggling writer, is
Frowned on by family and friends as a *'loafer'* in spite of his
Prodigious industry pounding night and day on his hired
Blickensdorfer typewriter while sacrificing food and
Cigarettes for paper, stamps and envelopes: *'Get a Job! Go to
Work! Poor, stupid slaves... obsessed by their own slavery.
A job was to them a golden fetish before which they fell down
And worshipped'*; there was a return to the *'doomed Keatsian'*
Concept of the writer, *'innately talented... preordained to
Sacrifice his health, and possibly sanity, in the quest to
Describe some final truth'* (Keats, lower-middle-class
Cockney, born to the sound of Bow Bells at the Swan and
Hoop pub in Moorgate, baptised at St Botolph-without-
Bishopsgate); one fictional *'doomed Keatsian'* was waifish
Edwin Reardon in George Gissing's *New Grub Street*;
*'The pervasiveness of this received idea... meant... young
Writers did sit writing into the night... unsupported by...
Political friends... producing a completely personal
Testimony... in spite of other people rather than in common
Cause with them... invoking'* the image of *'starving in a
Garret'*; Roland Camberton's blackly comical *Scamp* was
The *'archetypal novel'* of the *'deracinated writer'*: *'Ginsberg...
With another would-be writer, Bellinger, lives in... an
Apartment block in Bloomsbury 'collecting rejection slips"*
(Perennial trope – Martin Eden concludes: *'There was no
Human editor at the other end, but a... cunning arrangement
Of cogs that changed the manuscript from one envelope to
Another and stuck on the stamps'*); Alexander Baron's paling
Reputation was rescued – with Camberton's – by Worpole and
Others, posthumously recognised classics of the working-
Class canon, *Rosie Hogarth, King Dido*... Worpole closed on

A pessimistic note: *'Literature came too late to save politics.*
The connections had all been broken. The castle had been
Abandoned'... but never to be reoccupied? Perhaps, in part, by
The promise of blue-spined Pelicans and those working-class
Talents who filtered with them and filled the gentrified shelf
Of British reading matter with lean-tos of grittier literatures...

XXIII

Key in this reclamation of culture for the working classes,
Of course, was Hoggart's part-autobiographical monograph–
Poem-monograph to some – perceived by keen-eyed critics
To be a polemic criticising mass commercialism and creeping
Philistinism as cultural threats to the fraying legacy
Of wartime mutual improvement and opportunities amplified
By the post-war Attlee Settlement, a fertile ground from
Which had blossomed many upcoming working-class and
Lower-middle-class talents and which would culminate in
Michael Young's concept of an Open University which came
About under Harold Wilson's Labour Government in 1969;
Michael Young's dystopian polemic, *The Rise of the*
Meritocracy 1870–2033, first published 1958, reprinted by
Pelican 1961, was a partly fictive, time-travelling satirical
Polemic from the vantage-point of 2034, surveying
The culmination of meritocratic principles put in place in
British society decades before in the formation of a new elite
Supplanting the old nepotistic, inherited, privileged
Hegemonies on the basis of perceived intellectual merit via
The simple equation that IQ + effort = Merit, whilst
Neglecting other less logical intellectual talents and aptitudes,
Creativity and lateral thinking, and, in spite of many opposite
Impressions, Young was arguing against meritocracy, against
His own conceptual neologism – a misconstrued Canute
Of Cultural Studies: *'Education has put its seal of approval*
On a minority' thus creating simply another new elite
Superimposed upon the old, though one based on perceived

Merit; Young had helped draft the Labour Party's 1945
Manifesto *Let Us Face The Future* and in his polemic he did
Just that by projection; with Peter Willmott, Young also
Penned the seminal Pelican *Family and Kinship In East
London*, affectionately abbreviated by his peers to a cockney-
Inflected acronym *'Fakinel'*; Pelican imported many seminal
Left-of-centre cultural classics from across the pond: *The Sea
Around Us* by Rachel Carson, JK Galbraith's *The Affluent
Society*, Vance Packard's *The Naked Society* and *The Hidden
Persuaders* which both stealthily questioned the mythological
Mirage of the *'American dream'*; titles by Erving Goffman, Lewis
Mumford and Studs Terkel also appeared – but no
Jargon clogged this access to knowledge, no matter how
Esoteric the subject, prose always clear, precise, compendious
... Key to Pelicans' commercial success, their striking liveries
Displaying hallmarks of sharp-cornered Thirties art deco,
The original range with their *'iconic triband covers'* designed
By Edward Young –*'A bright splash of fat colour'* (as Allen
Lane called it) with a horizontal white band in the middle
Where author and title were displayed in angular Gill Sans;
And the emblem of the imprint, a flying pelican, on face and
Spine; post-war, Pelican covers were designed by ex-Bauhaus
Associate and Weimar Republic film poster designer, Jan
Tschichold, who mutated the template by inserting *'a central
White panel framed by a blue border'*; come the Sixties,
The liveries altered again, now containing cover illustrations
Under the designing eye of Milano Art Director, Germano
Facetti, a survivor of Mauthausen labour camp, who, as John
Walsh wrote, transformed the Pelicans *'from linear severity
And puritanical simplicity into a series of pictorial coups'* –
The covers of *The Stagnant Society* by Michael Shanks, those
By designers he recruited, Jock Kennier's take for Alex
Comfort's *Sex in Society*, Derek Birdsall's cover for
Vance Packard's *The Naked Society*, struck sparks... During
The Sixties Jenny Diski recounted taking out a subscription to '
*... the unofficial University of Pelican books course... Month
By month titles came out by Laing and Esterson, Willmott and
Young, JK Galbraith... each offering... latest thinking for an*

Unspecialised public, and the blue spines on the pile of books
On the floor of the bedsit increased... If you weren't at
University studying a particular discipline... Pelican books
Were the way to get the gist of things... anti-psychiatry, social
Welfare, economics, politics... sexual behaviour of young
Melanesians... the anatomy of this, that and the other,
The affluent, naked and stagnant society in which we found
Ourselves' – all thrown in to this didactic lucky dip!
Pelicans Were *Woolworths'* first, most pedagogic pick-and-mix;
Tapped into the thriving counterculture of that psychedelic
Decade, the radical imprint a kaleidoscope of topical polemic,
A progressively subversive university available to all; its
Sixties list included Hugo Thomas' *The Spanish Civil War*,
Erving Goffman's *Stigma: Notes on the Management of*
Spoiled Identity, Alasdair MacIntyre's *Marxism and*
Christianity, Charles Rycfort's *Anxiety and Neurosis* (both
'68), all published in 1969 – prime amongst this crop,
Professor JH Plumb's *The Death of The Past*, which, apart
From its main argument history is an ideological human
Concept superimposed upon the past (pace Walter Benjamin's
Axiom *'History is written by the victors'* – just as *'The history*
Of the poor is a history of attitudes to the poor'; Jeremy
Seabrook, *Pauperland*), also mused on eschatological and
Teleological entanglements of Christianity, and Marxism,
The latter seeking to ethically replace the former but which
Fell into its own contradictory cul-de-sac of chiliastic
Predilections and speculations as to an effective material
Afterlife on earth with the overthrow of capitalism and
'Dictatorship of the proletariat' (secular flipside
Of the thousand year rule of Christ and the Saints...?)
Through which *'class conflict will end'* and *'the state wither*
Away', Plumb arguing *'Marxist dialectic itself supposes an*
Ultimate end for the practical use of the past', which echoes,
By way of the most brutal examples, Stalinism's *'historical*
Cleansing' and Communism's ingrown religiousness –
'God-Building' – with tacit sanctification of still-living or past
National leaders as State Saints, Lenin prime example,
Embalmed in state so his waxen corpse – pickled in aspic

Of vodka and quinine to stop the skin's posthumous blotching
– Could attempt to perceptibly out-sleep perpetuity in its
Public glass sarcophagus as secular counterpoint to those
Uncorrupted corpses of sundry Catholic Saints, such as
That of Bernadette Soubirous of the grotto (and was there
Another unspoken reason why the baroque multi-coloured
Onion domes of St. Basil's were left intact and not
Demolished by Soviet planners, other than pure aesthetics?
Did even Soviet Communism have built-in obsolescence?);
Here implicitly and graphically was depicted an unconscious
Communist wish to cheat death or mimic some kind
Of immortality (didn't Gorky project humankind would
Eventually evolve into pure minds with vestigial bodies,
Dispensable residues peeled off, to become pilots of post-
Consciousness, ontological conquistadors?) – sugared
Almond demagogues; thus were the atheistic Comrades-in-
Chief sculpted into secular icons whilst still alive, visible
Living gods everyone could believe in, apotheosised emperors
Still corporeal, peasant-class tsars of the proletariat,
Omnipotent, omnipresent, as in the muscular, monolithic
Statues of the Stalin Cult, crypto-Olympians of a new
Agnostic mythology almost as superstitious and unworldly as
Religions it overgrew like weeds and yews in churchyards; so
Many triumphant Easter Island figures, granite Titans in
The end having eaten their own children, outlasted
Their obsessive builders after deforestation and wiping out all
Natural resources so they ended up in civil strife and starving,
All to construct stone icons, granite idols, flint-carved gods to
Stare out eternity without any worshippers, or like ancestral
Busts on stately mantelpieces gathering dust surrounded by
White-sheeted furniture – hence the perennial human cult
Of '*ancestor worship*', as Plumb picked up on, the primal
Need for humans to raise up the gene pool on pedestals,
Plinths and platforms, trace family trees back to much-hoped-
For blue or purple blood, or something near enough which at
Least merits a coat-of-arms, encompasses all peoples from
Rapa Nui and Bolsheviks to nouveaux riche Essex men hiring
Cut-price Bluemantle Pursuivant of Arms in Ordinary to

Create for them fake bespoke coats-of-arms, germinate
Bargain genealogies to help them emigrate from long-
Neglected egalitarian gains of bygone Attlee Settlements to
Post-Thatcherite aristocratisation of status on basis of material
Acquisitiveness, venal cultivation of received avarice,
Calvinistic anti-virtue, but, to non-believers – capitalist-
Apostates – a spiritually enervating vice, weighing in
Negative gains without educative leaven of intellectual yeast,
Or armature of cultural awareness, aesthetic curiosity; so
Philistinism is the indiscipline of a species of shopkeepers
Who worship episcopacies of packaging and brands at
Expense of authentic products, commodities made almost
Sentient with personalities projected into them by
Depersonalised shoppers, zombie consumers, and tulpa-like
Monopolies of mother-brands (capitalism worships goods not
Gods; commodity-gods); shopkeepers whose scriptures are
Advertising spiel and reels of receipts, whose sacraments are
Bricks and cement, stockpiling empty properties, never
Tempted by titles on sky-blue spines to partake in a spot
Of psychical self-improvement; these masses' primary aims,
It seems, self-betterment through bricks and motors rather
Than books and mortarboards, the only will to any levelling
Vented through voting in collective viewing of reality
Television and reification of real lives to virtual reels –
Commodity-fetishism (unpacked by Edmund Wilson in
The 'Karl Marx: Poet of Commodities' chapter in *To The
Finland Station*); a cultural race to the bottommost lowest
Common denominator of confected *Coronation Street* class-
Consciousness, bargain-basement inverted Bolshevism
Of blue-rinsed game for Bazalgette-bait (that blazing name
That brought us a central sewer system and, further down
The pipeline, reality television – ultimate anathema and
Nemesis of the original Reithian principles of public service
Broadcasting founded in the Thirties, to promote *'All that is
Best in every department of human knowledge, endeavour and
Achievement... The preservation of a high moral tone... of
Paramount importance'*, promulgated from Portland Place's
'Modernist citadel' which ruled all it surveyed with a *'hand*

Of granite' laying down the gauntlet, the BBC was since its
Inception – in spite of spin – implicitly political (and, once,
Left wing) and with its monopoly, supremely humble,
Unapologetically didactic – policed by philanthropic public
Intellectuals, highbrows, boffins, the Bertrand Russells and
Malcolm Muggeridges, satellites of altruistic intelligentsia,
Custodians of educational broadcasting, what might have led
To what 'Red' Ellen Wilkinson, when Education Secretary
Under Clement Attlee, envisioned as a *'third programme
Nation'*; later, such values would lead to the golden age in
British television in the Sixties and Seventies, groundbreaking
Social drama, Jeremy Sandford and Ken Loach's *Cathy Come
Home*, David Mercer's *Where The Difference Begins* and *In
Two Minds*, David Rudkin's visionary *Penda's Fen*, Don Taylor's
Marxist-allegorical ghost story *The Exorcism*, Jim Allen's
Days of Hope and *The Spongers* (directed by Roland
Joffé –both Allen and Joffé, members of the Workers'
Revolutionary Party in the Seventies thus sporadically
Blacklisted), *The Wednesday Play*, *Play For Today*, prolific
Costume dramas, painstaking literary adaptations, electric
Theatre, and once-ubiquitous Public Information Films,
Educational entertainment... But Thatcherism streamlined
Culture according to its philistine edicts, culminating in
Bazalgette barrel-scrapings of synthetic collectiveness and
Passive-receptive groupthink promoted through the almost-
Irresistible mob mentality of patriotism, sport and red-tops,
Mental prostration before inaccessible celebrities and parasitic
Royals known on first name terms courtesy of red-top
Chaperones, team-tribalism of footie, flag-painted faces on
Chanting terraces – Brittonic Iceni caterwauling a Hadrian's
Wall of Sound – gleaming with vicarious gratification at
Their tribe's goal-scoring, multi-millionaire players applauded
By cash-strapped supporters; such germs of self-flagellating
Allegiances relegated to amalgamates of Union Jack-waving
Jingoism whose engine was a strange melange of foreign
Intervention and Little Englandism, granting governments
Mandates warmongering and *'regime change'* – jingoism
Grown from greasy clothes and grimy streets of fin-de-siècle

East End slums, Arthur Morrison's Jago, the Old Nichol,
Brown-singed dog-end ghettoes little better in effect on mind
And body than barbed wired compounds pioneered by Herbert
Kitchener in the Boer War (another 'hero' of which, Robert
Baden-Powell, founded the Scout Movement piloted by
Jamboree on Brownsea Island); and clerks, white-collar
Corporals, oppressed by pressures of labour oversupply and
Piling unemployment prompted by commercial expansion and
Diminishing demand, took part in demonstrations of patriotic
Feeling and Jack-waving on news of the Reliefs of Ladysmith
And Mafeking – office workers who filled the ranks
As volunteer conscripts to fight in the veldt niftily through
Tent-flaps, now done up smart in khaki cloth and neck-
Curtains to cater to their chauvinism, some becoming non-
Commissioned officers, promoted two stripes to corporals...

XXIV

But cast back only a few decades, ordinary people were still
Partial to intellectual repasts, and Pelicans supplied these
Through a dazzling assortment of titles: Penelope Houston
Peter's *The Contemporary Cinema* introduced a generation
To the films of Bergman, Resnais, Truffaut; Laurie's *Drugs*,
Peter Mayer's *The Pacifist Conscience*, titles by AS Neill,
Roger Lewis, AJP Taylor, Herbert Marcuse et al... Pelican
Tackled history radically with Christopher Hill's re-depiction
Of the English Civil War as the English Revolution in
The World Turned Upside Down (its compendious
Introductions of hitherto obscure radical luminaries into
Pseudo-household names for contemporary scholars –
Gerrard Winstanley, John Lilburne, Joseph Salmon, Joseph
Bauthumley, Lawrence Clarkson, Roger Crab et al – and
Focus on 'Radical Madness', Puritan mad hatters,
Irrationalities of human personalities as covert expressions
Of political dissent, historically chiming with the anti-
Psychiatry of RD Laing pace *The Politics of Experience and*

The Bird of Paradise, taking Robert Burton's *The Anatomy of Melancholy* into the bargain), and, for Pelican's thousandth
Title, EP Thompson's seminal tome *The Making of The English Working Class*, which suited Pelican's ethos so
Implicitly through its voluminous focus on the history
Of Nonconformist mutual improvement among the labouring
Classes; Pelicans supplied leftfield literature upstream to
A growingly sophisticated proletariat, cheaply priced supplies
On cheap paper but with always arresting Modernist cover
Designs, seemed no stopping this imprint pumping out from
Its print salvos easily digestible food for permanent
Revolutions in thought continuing... until... after a suitably
Provocative run throughout the last ditch decade of British
Social democracy and establishment-questioning, the nerve-
Verged, ragged-edged Seventies – *Poverty: The Forgotten Englishman* by Ken Coates and Richard Silburn (a polemic
With schematic aspects reminiscent of Mass Observation,
Blistering indictment – based on surveys of slum districts in
Nottingham – of the Beveridgean welfare blueprint being
Mostly about damage-limiting unemployment and poverty
Rather than comprehensively alleviating them, documenting
How the British State ever dished out dole with more
A clenched fist than open palm), *Superman and Common Man – Freedom, Anarchy and The Revolution* by Benjamin
R Barber (in which democracy was criticised for amounting to
Little more than '*majoritarianism*', crypto-tyrannical rule by
A majority, or '*mob*', mostly brainwashed by politically
Biased tabloids to invariably vote Right; while anarchism was
Depicted as trans-materialism, a movement of imagination,
Appealing most to recalcitrant aristocratic thinkers and
Writers, whereas Marxism was ultimately as materialist as
Capitalism which it sought to supplant – slightly
Disingenuous given the very countervailing motives),
The Language of Madness by David Cooper... the Pelican
Brand was gradually abraded by the grab-happy Eighties
Finally spluttering its last at the fag-end of that streamlined
Decade with its 2,878th title, William Sheridan Allen's
The Nazi Seizure of Power, the imprint discontinued by 1990

…Why? Perhaps due to a toxic combination of the new
Thatcherite men-in-suits' more corporate approach to
Publishing, and emerging germ of postmodernism, contagious
Deconstructionism, catching – by the sounds of it – on
The antennae of at least one Penguin spokesman who quipped
That the Pelican logo was now seen as a symbol denoting
'This book is a bit worthy' – since when was *'worthy'* such
A terrible thing? Since postmodernism scooped out the point
From expression and criticism in order to try and prove
Everything is relative, ultimately subjective, intrinsically
Ironic, endlessly reductive – now there's only hope in
The New Sincerity… So Pelican became an extinct sub-
Imprint but continued to circulate second-hand through
Charity bookshops, still cheaply priced but much prized and
Since their original production runs were so vast there was
Never a shortage of its thousands of titles, so ubiquitous those
Blue spines they became staples of book-recycling
Enterprises, a good few dozen made available for second and
Third readerships every time a war baby or baby boomer died
Leaving behind their own rockpool-sample of blue-spined
Primers, their own humble well-thumbed numbered libraries
For left-leaning amateur scholars, students, shabby bohemian
Browsers, and nostalgic writers with a taste for dog-eared
Commentaries from obsolete social democracies beckoning
Them back to gentler times of more questioning minds with
Imaginative ambition, progressive verve preserved in
Nostalgia's isinglass yet seemingly so ahead not only
Of their time, but even of future times in which they
Resurfaced, woodchipped optimism for a future human
Flourishing seeming to them almost inevitable from such
Fertile earth of well-tilled, long-ploughed, soul-nourishing
Thought but which would be abruptly tramped down by
Grinding engines of Eighties' self-gain in tangibles, get-rich-
Quick, dog-eat-dog, law of the jungle instant gratification –
With Thatcherism there was only mock-trickledown
Extremely limited to a select portion of the working classes,
Forming a new consumer population, blue collars, skilled
Manual workers, nouveau riche, but no cultural trickledown

Accompanied this bare bones *embourgoisement*, no
Governmental encouragement of greater learning and
Knowledge-gathering, because Margaret Thatcher wanted her
New consumer population politically compliant and
Sociologically ignorant so as not to threaten the new
Economic hegemony, unfettered free market catastrophically
Unleashed with the stock market Big Bang of 1986 which
Deregulated greed, such philistinism part and parcel
Of the Thatcherite creed, for Socialism cannot flourish amid
The rusty tins and discarded cans of capitalist junk culture...
But who's to read this new species of Pelicans? Who's to be
Its new breed of readership? The already-converted middle-
Class Primrosian metropolitan commentariat, members
Of whom also number among its authorships? Can these new
Pelicans somehow pierce a common readership? Turn
The (invariably) shaven heads of Boris's breed of blue-collar
Conservatives? Can hermetically sealed, atavistic, solvent
Sun And *Daily Express*-reading white van SatNav man, jingoistic
'Gammon', technologically-caged Cro-Magnon, turn his
Attention span to consuming some paperback Marxism or
Myth-busting of capitalism, morph into a sympathetic army
Of plain-clothed anxious corporals? Can Pelicans promote
Those happily manipulated red top-dependents to two stripes
Of opinion and perception...? while diehard bleeding-hearted
Socialists, Communists and progressives continue to fight for
Emancipation of a kind of working class which no longer
Exists (or, if it does, doesn't *know* it does), having long since
Been atomised along with manufacturing, or who don't want
To be emancipated from encapsulated push-button open
Prison complexes of escapism, or for the future dictatorship
Of an ectopic proletariat sponsored by News Corp to despise
The poor, unemployed and disabled, shadows-at-one-remove
Of themselves, so become their own oppressors, prison-
Keepers, their own pawnbrokers; patrolling their own post-
Proletarian parameters of morality by meting out rough
Musickings to rough sleepers, Skimmingtons of *'scrounger'*-
Calling contrapuntal to red-tops' daily clamour against benefit
Claimants and immigrants, and *'Chav'* charivaris, mocking

Outcasts of their own class, the new workless classes cast out
Into sink-estates, not entirely unlike travellers in their outskirt
Reservations, and Gypsies stigmatised by Nimby-burgesses
And vigilantes buzzing on anti-ziganism – yet all stripes
Of proletarian sink in swamps of parochialism, some because
Impoverishment traps them materially within shrinking
Boundaries, stagnant breeding grounds for germs of ennui,
Moral miasmas, soups of apathy, where there's neither
Perceived point to changing the world nor even interpreting it,
Just *'putting up'*... Perhaps we should be more optimistic, in
The spirit of Pelican's original principles, that in these austere
Times, these second Thirties retconned by rhetoric, this
Depression reprise when the welfare state is being dismantled
Piece by piece, and trebled university fees are putting higher
Education ever further out of reach of the lower-middle and
Working classes, ever more expensive degrees increasingly
Monopolised by sons and daughters of privilege, campuses
Privatised, the Arts all but bought-up by the nepotistic upper
Echelons and their heirs apparent, old school ties of private
Education and Oxbridge regaining their grip, knowledge
Gentrified, and much focus on science and technology in
Order to make for a more *'competitive'* future workforce –
In spite of the march of automatism and the fringe-proposition
Of a rational adaptation to a future post-work society, in
A universal basic income – those seeking a more rounded
Education who cannot afford the fees, can now at least
Unceremoniously enrol in pop-up Pelican Universities;
Subscribing to this new species of outré instruction might not
Lead to a scroll or certificate of official qualification but it can
Furnish disenfranchised minds – forced through a reining-in
Of ringfencing and sifting nets to rusticate and gather rust in
Pauperising apprenticeships, underemployment, unpaid work
Placements and zero-hours contracts – with leftfield
Foundations, and through such a vicarious invisible university
Time might invest in a disadvantaged but talented young
Enlivened by an alternative worldview to conventional
Education, an outcast cognoscenti collecting in alfresco
Colleges, germinals for marginalia of marginalised and

Marshalling of arguments, a caucus of autodidacts more
Cultured and intellectually eclectic than privileged graduates
Dripped with received knowledge on conveyor-belts,
Academic assembly lines, and might eventually revolutionise
The drives of the underprivileged to advance themselves as
Savants of a new more imaginative age, indigo children in no
Need of degrees, an invigorated aggregate of sociological
Knowledge mingled in ranks of a burgeoning self-educated
Precariat self-trained to ask awkward questions as to cheated
Inheritances, who might populate polarised poor districts and
Doughnut ghettoes with new supplies of anxious corporals to
Occupy the spaces left empty by complacency of sponsored
Auspices, anxious corporals to lap up apocryphal scholarship
From peripheral hemispheres of human understanding and
Perception, anxious corporals of a new ectopic rupture in
A sharply apprehensive and sceptical proletariat appreciative
That their collective identity has been appropriated by powers
That be to keep employers supplied with a surplus of cheap
Labour and red tops and politicians with a perpetual pool
Of unemployed scapegoats, the most exceptional and
Intellectually entrepreneurial of whom might start piloting
Corresponding societies, discussion groups, workshop
Cooperatives, mutual improvement societies, like those
Of the equally lacklevel Victorian times, which produced such
Perceived proletarian upstarts as The Black Lamp, Chartists,
Tolpuddle Martyrs, Peterloons, more than simply postscripts
To their class but pioneers and protestors who developed
Incipient *'working-class consciousness'* which caught on
Nascent English socialism to dovetail with middle-class
Gradualist Fabianism and form the Labour Party, first led by
Ex-miner and autodidact, near-mythic James Keir Hardie –
And these self-educative influences filtered through fingers
Of aspiring proletarian poets and writers, leveller versifiers,
Versifying weavers, peasant poets through the prolific crop
Of Chartist Bards up to the 'Super-Tramp' WH Davies,
Their shadow-lineage of autodidactic traceries reflected in
Fiction from the Yellow Nineties (America's Mauve Decade)
Through the turn-of-the-century in such literary folkloric

Characters as Felix Holt, Jude Fawley, Martin Eden –
Iconoclastic icons of socialistic consciences intricately latticed
With contradictory misanthropies and bohemian
Rebelliousness towards established mores of their times...

XXV

Occasionally a socialistic consciousness crept in and out
Gaining more of the shore incrementally as recrudescent tides
Driven by restive waves aggrieved by profit-motives,
Whisperings of restlessness stretching out across parched
Sands thirsting cultural replenishment, appetites which spiked
In the Depression when scarcity wasted material tastes on
Sour mouths and dry throats of capitalism's streptococcal
Implosion and the slap and purl of impecuniousness in
The wakes of the Wall Street Crash and a backwash
Of capitalist apostasy in its aftermath, when more authentic
Riches such as the polished apples of scholarship appeared to
Carry more currency in the intellectual sense, ripe fruit for
The picking, cheap and accessible produce purchasable under
The Pelican imprint for a mere sixpence a pinch, plenty
Of cultural supply for the pinched, cash-strapped, hard-
Pressed, apron-stringed pin money, cheaply priced supplies
For a common readership of priceless prose polemics in
Common ownership, no more need for scrumping now apples
Dropped in the hand... Will contemporary Pelicans have such
A common reach or will they simply fill a niche? As Paul
Laity speculated in a *Guardian* piece, *'No doubt Penguin's
Aim is to capitalise on the now-fetishised Pelican brand'*, just
As it has on its own brand's iconic designs reproduced on
Mugs, coasters, postcards, tea-towels, through Thirties and
Forties retro chic of recent times, the *KEEP CALM AND CARRY
ON* blitz-nostalgia of lightning austerity; precarious
Sales pitch which could see Pelicans become inadvertent
Victims of their own commodity-fetishism (ultimate coup
Of capitalism) their blue spines status symbols of cultural

Currency, but merely symbols, like money, on otherwise
Sparsely populated suburban bookshelves ('Laurence: *[puts The Shakespeare volume back on the bookshelf]* Our nation's
Culture... Not something you can actually read, of course' –
Abigail's Party, 1977) – O Suburbia, Betjeman's iambic limbo
Of bungalows and shrubberies, stout Thirties' semi-detacheds,
Bay-windowed incubators of hobby-abated boredom sporting
Front parlours and trophy rooms, lace-curtained
'*Respectability*', scope for polemical prowling by poetic
Interlopers – paid sardonic homage by poet-and-shopkeeper
Harold Monro in his bristling 'Aspidistra Street'...

Sure, the lovely fools who made Utopia
Planned it without any aspidistra.
There will be a heaven on earth, but first
We must banish from the parlour
Plush and poker-work and paper flowers,
Brackets, staring photographs and what-nots,
Serviettes, frills and etageres,
Anti-macassars, vases, chiffonniers;

And the gloomy aspidistra
Glowering through the window-pane,
Meditating heavy maxims,
Moralising to the rain.

Upended by Orwell's hapless Gordon Comstock stalked by
Aspidistras in '*respectable*' lodgings – pot-plants which,
In domestic ubiquity were almost as disturbing as Wyndham's
Triffids– briefly absconded from by George Bowling on
A day trip down memory lane to Lower Binfield, coming up
For air like a carp from a pond; to think true bouleversement
Of stratums was bought off by labyrinths of boulevards and
Mazes of avenues (invariably named picturesquely after
Various poets perceived to have been too subversive,
Bohemian and immoral to be permitted as tangible
Neighbours), privet hedges, mock-classical villas and
Gravelled drives – columned homes increasingly inhabited

By uncultivated minds, as Hoggart elaborated: '*Self-made men*
Now living in villas – grocers who have done well and own
A small chain of local shops; jobbing builders who have
Advanced so far as to be putting up fields of private 'semis''
But who still '*like to join the crowd at football matches*' in
Their '*Harris tweed*'; gardened suburbs, '*miniature Arcadias*'
As S Martin Gaskell called them, dreamt up by empty
Sleepers, ended up an unenvied nouveaux-riche leitmotiv in
'*Villadom*', avenues for parvenus, arriviste drives, solvent
Villas, vulgarian gardens, habitats of prosaic consciousness,
Uncultivated taste, cultureless, uncurious; soon to scoop up
More greenbelt in a remorseless suburban grab and expansion
Of commuter belts combing ruggedly picturesque brownfield
Wastelands, authentic outskirts of lace-curtained civilisation
Where feral children, charvees, gypsies, Roma and urban
Foxes were rumoured to roam... Gradually these outlands
Colonised by prefabricated bricks of inferior quality in what
Became known as '*the spoiling of the suburbs*', whereby
Originally signature gardened realms of well-remunerated
Middle classes were growingly ringed by commingling lower-
Middle- and upper-working classes migrating to the outer
Rims; a gradual process of demographic outgrowth from
Urban conurbations begun when the upwardly mobile middle
Class, according to Geoffrey Crossick in his *The Lower*
Middle Class In Britain, 1870–1914 (1979) '*snatched*
The crumbs from the rich man's table, colonising any part of
The outskirts not already bespoken by the very well-to-do'
Around the 1880s, sniffing out affordable foundations, what
Building News termed '*those trim semi-detached villas and*
Terraces that soon make their appearance when the demand
Arises' – some of which were let as nursing homes, private
Asylums, schools; by the 1900s, '*whole districts were being*
Transformed from quaint hillsides into red blotches, while
The Ecclesall Road was being converted into respectable
Villadom', labyrinths of *rus-in-urbe* or at least its semblance –
The best that could be bought or rented by green-fingered
Lower-middle-class clerical workers housed in close
Proximity to the working class who tended bruised allotments

Nearby; but those travelling through would observe how
Arcadian villas eventually gave way to serried *'Respectable'*
Terraces, which, as Crossick described, *'abutted in turn, often
With surprising suddenness, on to established works in...
Valleys and densely congregated back-to-back housing'*,
Stratified streets that put Charles Booth's class-descriptive
Maps into sharp relief, bands of A, B, C: A for *'professionals
And shopkeepers'*, B and C for *'respectable and hardworking
Artisans'*... The A band was particularly broad a stratum since
Shopkeepers were steeply stratified up and down the pyramid
Of what Thea Vigne and Alun Howkins called *'shopocracy'* –
The hierarchy of shopkeeping – which ranged from
The corporation *'barons'* at the top, the likes of Gordon
Selfridge, right down to the shabby corner shops with
Curtained-off backrooms, some of them *'small cramped
Stores usually kept by disabled miners or widows'* as Janet
Cheadle of Bolton noted of her own origins, or parlour-shops,
Those that occupied the dowdy front rooms of family homes,
And while these small-time shopkeepers occupied a certain
Position in the community power structure, even sometimes
Serving as temporary moneylenders until customers' paydays
Or providing provisions on tabs for the in-between-wages-
Days, as those of Salford's working-class district of Hankey
Park – wherefrom Walter Greenwood, autodidact author
Of *Love On The Dole*, hailed – but whose *'power brought
With it no trappings of social prestige'*, seen as no better or
Posher than their customers; nonetheless some of them
Perceived local shopkeepers as socially superior, such as one
Mr Doyle who belonged to *'the respectable working men's
Class but on the poor side'* who thought the shopkeepers
Of his district *'was the only upper class I knew'*, and even
Some members of the white-collar lower-middle classes saw
Shopkeepers as districts' *'dukes and duchesses'*, but most
Benevolent *'Nobs'* – as opposed to *'snobs'* – of noblesse
Oblige, most obliging, patriarchal in approach, especially at
Christmas and New Year when *'everybody got an orange off
Every shop'*; some shopkeepers donated items to the Guilds
Of Help and Clog Funds; other customers differed in

Perceptions of shopkeepers, seeing them as *'snobs and toffs'*
Of their communities; for the working classes most was
Purchased on credit, or club cards, nothing actually owned,
And shopkeepers *'provided the tick whereby you lived... even
The clothes you wore were on the tick – they were on credit,
Nothing bought for cash'*; shops were community hubs:
*'The paper-shop window is a litter of odds-and-bobs...
Frame-full of sixpence-a-week advertisements... makes an
Exchange and mart... full of items 'in v.g. condition''...*
Shopkeepers often perceived as microscopic capitalists, adept
At adapting to circumstances and environments, brown-
Coated grocers-cum-social Darwinists, supremely pragmatic,
Class-camouflaged among goods they kept the common
Touch, hence weren't seen as a cut above, unlike white-collar
Workers whom Boltonians of Selford Park saw as snobs,
'Anybody who worked in an office was a bit above you' while
Rent collectors were chaps *'with a parlour and a piano'* –
Pace LS Lowry; bigger shopkeepers especially in the sticks
Were seen, according to Crossick, as *'pillars of Respectability
And the sociologists' ideal bourgeois'*, while somewhere in
Between were *'tally men and agents'* of the department stores
In country towns, often magnified in eyes of visiting villagers
As great bustling cities, as Jude saw Christminster's spires, or
One Joseph Ashby of the village of Tysoe perceived Banbury
As reminiscent of a giant fair in the Russian city of Nijni
Novgorod of which he'd read in a schoolbook – but these
Country towns also had their slums of crammed tenements
Strung with washing lines, doorsteps sprung with filthy
Children; there was the *'slum shop'* as depicted by Alice Foley in
A Bolton Childhood, a particular one run by one Charlie
Clifton whose shop scrubbed up into a social club for
Locals, and who being *'the type of man... he'd had the sort of
Education'* would write letters on behalf of illiterate
Customers in disputes and arguments, a shopkeeper who just
About got by in spite of low profit margins, who had much
Sympathy for those trapped in *'the vagaries of employment'*
And how wages could strain family budgets, whose prices
Were always bespoke depending on customers' abilities to

Pay, *'A pennorth of candles, three candles for a penny'*, say;
There was sometimes room for bartering from shopkeeper-to-
Shopkeeper, exchanges of goods without money changing
Hands, *'settling up touch'*; Mr Clifton's daughter, a Mrs
Lovell, recalled her mother's sense of dislocation from her
Working-class neighbours, since she was from a shabby-
Genteel background, had *'a strong sense of Respectability'*
And *'stifled part of her nature'*, *'... she couldn't really be
Herself, she liked poetry... when you're in Rome you do
The same as Rome does... probably she was... bottled up'* –
While politics was a no-no; thus were the Cliftons *'ill at ease
In the community, conscious of the narrow divide between
Them and their customers'*, as narrow as the shabby curtain
That screened off the shop's backroom where the family *'ate
Their meals'* at one partitioned remove; Gallichan of course
Had much to say on the shopkeeper breed in his
Blight of Respectability: *'See the poor mercantile clerks... shopmen,
The genteel drudges... Guy de Maupassant picture the type:
'Poor threadbare devils who vegetate frugally in a... little
Plaster-house, with a flower bed for a garden"* –
Exasperatedly: *'How can we inveigh against these tired
Workers for the drowsy occupation of their few leisure hours?
... chiefly at fault is the crushing system that leaves so little
Time for expansion of the mind and... sympathies'*; Grant
White described a *'shopkeeping pair'* in his *England Without
And Within* whose faces were *'a greasy witness of content'*;
Gallichan continued rhetorically: *'Were there not originally...
Germs of ideas, imagination... in these unfortunate contented
Souls? Are such doomed to take no thought for higher things
Than bread-getting and eating, and will their minds for ever
Starve on the Bethel hymn and the newspaper?'*... Gallichan
Tackled the *'commercial ideal'*: *'... it is only when the shop
Absorbs the best of us'* that *'a man's moral sense and intellect
Are... warped'* inclining him towards *'the lower gratifications
Of life'*, which begged the question: *'Need money-getting
Always degrade...?'* need it *'be alone compatible with a
Corrupt canon of commercial morals?'* – mostly it would,
Reaching its apotheosis just over eighty years later in

The ideological reign of an Oxford-educated shopkeeper's
Daughter; *'The trader who makes Mammon his idol... and*
Spends his wealth irrationally, brutalises life. But... let us...
Pity... those who cannot... 'leave the shop.'', while noting
Exceptions: *'There are strong-minded... tradesmen who can*
Shake off the dust of the warehouse, and spend the hours of
Freedom in the cultivation of the intellect' but *'the merchant*
Who... murmurs a rhythm of Tennyson while he is at
The ledger, will... be an indifferent money-maker' (cue Robert 'Tea
Leaf' Clemesha, shopkeeper-poet, who composed poems
Politely chasing up customers for unpaid tabs, or asking
Friends for loans); in rhetorical mode once more: *'Is there no*
Escape from... bare affairs of the shop?... We have to
Determine... whether we shall aid... production of mediocre
Shopkeepers... or... rear a class who place business first and
Culture last'; Gallichan, nascent anti-capitalist, asserted he'd
'Rather live in a country of moderately prosperous men, who
Read and had aspirations... higher than lucre, than where
The mass were rich and unintellectual'... None could escape
Doing privet-time: *'We have to live in Villadom at some time*
... in our lives', as in Ashbourne Crescent in George Moore's
A Drama in Muslin, with its *'white-capped maidservants, and*
Spotless oilcloths' where *'there is... aversion to all... which*
Might disturb... the routine of existence', where Sunday dusks
Cast genteel silhouettes *'When the skies are flushed with*
Sunset, and the outlines of this human warren grow harshly
Distinct – black lines upon pale red'; Mortimer warned
Of the *'miasma of Villadom'* emphasising deathly attributes,
Its facilitation of anti-life and stasis, artificial suspension
Of personality, moribund banality, crushing mediocrity,
Elective philistinism against which Gallichan sharpened his
Darts of rhetoric: *'What does Villadom read, talk of, and think*
Upon?... fathers read the newspapers... mothers and
Daughters peruse John Halifax, and... literature of the Pap-
Boat and Pumplighter Sort' (or *'Galsworthy-and-water stuff'* –
Orwell), *'talk is of... the back-parlour window curtains and*
Carpets'; Gallichan incredulous to pathetic excuses for lack
Of cultivation: *'The denizens of Villadom tell you... they have*

Their livings to earn... houses to control' that *'there is no time*
For cultivating their intellects... No time! ...plea of the men
And women who squander hours in tittle-tattle and loafing' –
Yet, as Gallichan cited, there had been legion self-educating
Working-class souls whose strenuous efforts to lift themselves
Above circumstances, cultivate talents and gain wider
Knowledge to put the bourgeoisie to shame: *'Gerald Massey,*
A bargeman's son, and... fag in a factory; Elihu Burritt, a
Blacksmith; Thomas Edward, a shoemaker; Walt Whitman,
Compositor; Bradlaugh, a soldier, and afterwards a clerk...
Found time to read, and think, and improve themselves. It is
The will... not the leisure, that is lacking in Villadom'; thus
Villadom is enervating of human spirit and intellect, it is
'The end of civilised beings... Primitive barbarians... at least,
Wish to learn higher arts of living. No past civilisation
Presents this picture of philistine apathy' as illustrated in
'Crowds of... women standing, rapt in... admiration of bits of
Ribbon in... drapery stores'; Gallichan might well have said,
Via alliterative rhetorical device, Villadom was Vassaldom to
Conventionality... Villadom became ever more pervasive into
The early twentieth century – as charted compendiously by
Crossick, the 1920s saw sprung toadstools of *'parlour-*
Houses', terrace-sized alternatives to fatter semi-detacheds
Which could only be extended by building upwards into third
Storeys or installing attics, or back-extensions of kitchens or
Sculleries – *'The result of this type of layout was that all such*
Houses suffered from... long and dark internal passages, and
... limited... circulation of air and... admission of sunlight';
The marker buoy of suburban status was *'a bay window of at*
Least one storey' as Harold Dyos acknowledged, 'de rigueur
In all grades of housing by the end of 19th century', though as
S Martin Gaskell elaborated: *'Beyond this there was... scope*
For... decoration of stone sills and copings... the addition to
Porches... of columns with machine-turned capitals;
The insertion of coloured... bricks and moulded plasterwork;
The embellishment of forecourts with coloured tiles', this
Status-consciousness was also reflected in the interior:
'The imitation marble fireplace... floral wallpapers... bulky,

Veneered furniture... careful display of ornaments', as
Described in such contemporaneous samplers as Mr. Pooter's
In the Grossmiths' *Diary of A Nobody*, or SF Bullock's
Robert Thorne who comments on the symbolic trappings
Of his house: *'We were finding our feet in the social world,
Making the best show we could. The brass knocker* [and] *bay
Window... establish the fact'*; Crossick continued: *'Outside
The house, the intricacy of the cast iron railings and...
Variations in the planting of the front garden were...
Distinctive of different grades of respectability'* and *'the very
Naming of the streets'* was *'a subtle acknowledgement of
A locality's status in suburban society"*; such architectural
'Respectability' of bespoke abodes was often guilty
Of plagiarising features of better-heeled properties,
Of *'elaborating... bay window, gable, half-timbering, and
Ingle-nook'*; so much of the natural environment was
Sacrificed to achieve these effects: *'The ruthless despoliation
Of nature on the estate meant the cutting down of all trees
And... the formation of roads at extremely narrow intervals,
Bordered by identical redbrick houses with contracted
Passages and small rooms facing... the thoroughfare'*;
Common or garden character, garden varieties of villas –
Eruptions of utopian sentiments were thought to have
Contributed to this Arcadian character in architecture,
Cooperative societies and the Association for Improving
The Conditions of the People, and other amalgamates
Of gradualism, all attempting to bring middle-class values
Of thrift, hard work and saving to the thinning masses;
Redbrick estates increasingly became habitats of skilled
Artisans, master craftsmen, *'clerks, schoolmasters and
Shopkeepers'*, while the influence of the Arts and Crafts
Movement on architectural matters saw attempts to refurbish
And reassert primitive authority of workman's cottages, and
A gradualist reimagining of alms houses; then moved on to
Focusing on *'spatial qualities... the straight street of... terrace
Discarded in favour of the picturesque settlement of trees and
Gardens, with houses built semi-detached'* which would
Become most fashionable in the Twenties, Thirties, Forties;

While *'the roads had lost the rigidity of the gridiron'*, houses
Sprouted complementarily to close-combing curved tree-lined
Streets, crescents, closes, cul-de-sacs; new mixed-class
Communities transplanted in place of obsolete mutually
Excluding ones, *'by means of tenant co-partnership... ultimate
Refinement of Victorian self-help'*, eventually consolidated in
The Tenants Co-partnership Society; Charles Masterman
Noted how numerous Edwardian writers *'bore witness'* to
Suburbia's *'noticeable absence of vision'* – synthetic Arcadia,
As in JB Priestley's rumbled *Laburnum Grove*; HG Wells
And George Gissing (*In the Year of The Jubilee*) wrote
Of *'infinite boredom'* in *'expanding suburbs'*, Grossmith and
Bullock bore witness to *'its pettiness'* – one-upmanship was
The serpent in the garden suburb... Since the upper-working-
Cum-lower-middle classes, plagued by the embourgeoisement
Bug, the gentrifying germ, antsy with status anxieties –
Attempters in forming an angst-amalgamate of middle-class
Social and moral meanings among marginal groupings; thus
Susceptible to acquisitive viruses which broke out in pustules
Of competitiveness and one-upmanship prizing above all else
'Respectability' supported by self-respect; Gallichan had
Deconstructed all of this in his *Blight of Respectability*, which
Picked apart hypocrisies and foibles fostered in the *'frowsty
Atmosphere'* of net-curtained suburbia, venting his contempt
For it and everything it represented – *'Can any wholesome
Influence come out of... a villa inhabited by veneerings?'* – by
Verbally disembowelling the burgeoning breed
Of *'Respectables'* as *'Censors of genius... founders of public
Taste... friends of morality'* who think themselves *'capable of
Deciding* [that] *Shelley and Burns were 'immoral'...
Respectability makes Britain* [a] *laughing-stock...
The Respectables' stupid... 'patriotism' and bullying
Arrogance cause us to be hated in all quarters of the world'*;
Patriotism was the conservative collectivist equivalent to
Socialism, but unlike socialism focused not on economic
Conditions and the actual people of the nation but on notions
Of empire as an expansion of the sovereign venerated lump
Of land; imperialism markedly opposed to Little Englandism;

Patriotism was progenitor of jingoism, its muggier relation,
More belligerent tribal expression; both patriotism and
Jingoism were piston and engine of the Express of Empire –
Map-pinking epidemic of international exploitation and
Plundering, no respecter of precarious statuses of its office-
Bound patriotic supporters back home, mere supplementals,
Replaceable *'respectables'* displaced uncomplainingly into
Less important or permanent positions in spite of still
Benefiting from ripening domestic fruits, and happy, in any
Case, to still be brushing shiny-suited shoulders with social
Superiors – as Richard Price put it: *'Thus, imperialism was
Both... begetter and... albatross of the lower middle classes'*;
While *'patriotism provided one answer to... status insecurities
Of 'funny little people... groping in the dark'*, as Shan F
Bullock phrased it in *Robert Thorne: The Story of A London
Clerk*... Anxious corporals of social expectations who sought
The opposite to socialists, to draw up the status-ladder after
Them, define themselves and their material improvement by
Superior stations to those beneath them, and clinch
The capitalist pact by voting Conservative on every occasion
Presented them – hence *'Judases of Capitalism'*; as
Masterman intoned, *'in feverish hordes... suburbs swarm to...
Polling booths to vote against a truculent proletariat'* – put
Up bollards and barricades of ballot boxes to forever block
The way for Bolshevism... It has to be hoped today's
Deconstructed proletariat of the Twenty Twenties will not be
Content to be shopkeepers – as a certain *'Little Corporal'*
Once nicknamed the English, O Napoleon Bonaparte had
A penchant for aphorisms! – but will – along with
The reconstructed lapsed middle-class 'precariat', Bachelors
Of Arts Baristas – come to be keepers of soul-unlocking
Knowledge, catch up the cultural lag of a dragged-out
Gainsaying age of angst and austalgia, and once again come
To acknowledge that more lasting fruits are gained through
Learning than earning; that true power, self-empowerment
Comes through unsponsored scholarship, the impetus to self-
Improvement, mutual improvement, individuals coming
Together through collective endeavour of fellow travellers,

Those distance-learning autodidacts who craved educations
Uncensored and books unabridged; here is the hope for an
Aspiring readership to lap up and appreciate a new species
Of Pelicans to help emancipate hearts and minds from prisons
Of circumstances and provide alternative narratives on times
Past, present, future to those trumpeted by twin philistine
Heffalumps of capitalism: misanthropic red-top populism and
Two Nations Toryism that trump our spirits and trample our
Times... Or perhaps some hope lies in the lumpenproletariat,
Recomposing pools of compendiously oppressed peoples
Tipped out from fraying safety nets of a deflated welfare state
Onto scrapheaps of lost opportunities, with no stakes in
Society, those scapegoats called legion names – *'scroungers'*,
'Spongers', *'parasites'*, *'deadbeats'*, *'hobos'*, *'reprobates'*
Etc. – but who include literate street outcasts pitched on
Pavements of metropolises, thirsty not just for sustenance but
Authenticity – something which, no matter how drastic,
Parched and depersonalising, they attain after protracted time
Sitting static watching slurping slipper-feet of shop-
Hypnotised passers-by – anticipation of what promises to be
For all of us a post-corporeal oceanic consciousness like that
Feeling Arthur Koestler (very same coiner of the phrase
'Anxious corporals') – for one of infinite minds – experienced
During most perilous moments in his life, which he
Speculated might typify an afterlife, *'a de-personalised after-
Life beyond due confines of space, time and matter and
Beyond the limits of our comprehension'*, a bigness of soul
Swimming out unlimitedly without frontiers imposed by
Temporal personality or fetters of self (in its mortal
Adumbration, self-fragmentation, or ego-death – pace
RD Laing's Penguins) – for those psychiatry calls schizophrenic
And psychotic for surely any afterlife worth its salt would be
Implicitly Communist; they the only constant, rooted stones in
The daily fetishist stream of rushing humanity – and a more
Transcendent understanding of existence above materiality,
Turn at ever more frequent intervals to silent trickles
Of the written page, and in those captivating lakes
Of meaning-making, of careful thought and crafted phrase,

Empathic pools of escape, come to expand their mental plains
– Scuffed corporals of the pavements, many army veterans
Among them, Afghanistan-traumatised, Iraq-deracinated,
Some still coat-hangered in sand-coloured fatigues, psychical
Casualties of Middle East interventionism, amputees of new
Imperialism, collecting pennies in empty paper cups from
Starbucks, American-ground Arabic beans – having left
Behind empty helmets to be taken up by new recruits
Replacing them, strange characterless round metal helmets,
Nothing so strikingly designed as curved neck-shading pith
Helmets of old colonial campaigns, and certainly not as
Light... If some of them are lucky, they might be promoted up
To two stripes from pavement to halfway house or shelter or
A vending pitch touting for *'A hand up not a hand out'*...
Look! There, one such, his grimy fingers gripping a cracked
Pale blue spine of charity shop surplus – he's entranced,
Immersed in his inner-flow, his inner flourishing rushing in
Him, flooding his senses, seeping into his perception,
Enraptured by the Pelican's special present for receptiveness
With nothing to receive – see how he perches the paperback:
Hand up, palm supine...

Acknowledgements

My gratitude to Ken Worpole for his permission to excerpt as much as I wished from his brilliant *Dockers and Detectives*; to Alan Price for bringing to my attention the article 'Richard Hoggart and the Waning of the Working Class' by Jeremy Seabrook in *New Society*, 1982.

Sources

Dockers and Detectives: Popular Reading: Popular Writing Ken Worpole (Verso, 1983)

The Lower Middle Class ion Britain, 1870–1914

Geoffrey Crossick (Croom Helm Ltd., 1979)

Angels in Marble: Working Class Conservatives in Urban England Robert T. McKenzie & Allan Silver

(Heinemann Educational Publishers, 1968)

The Uses of Literacy: Aspects of Working-Class Life

Richard Hoggart (Chatto & Windus 1957; Pelican 1958)

The Blackcoated Worker: A Study in Class Consciousness

David Lockwood (George Allen & Unwin, 1958)

The Blight of Respectability: An Anatomy of The Disease and A Theory of Curative Treatment Walter M. Gallichan (as Geoffrey Mortimer) (The University Press Ltd., 1897)